FIRE YOUR FINANCIAL ADVISOR

FIRE YOUR FINANCIAL ADVISOR℠

40 YEARS OF GREED & EXPLOITATION OF THE AMERICAN RETIREE

AND HOW YOU CAN FIGHT BACK

GREG ALER

LIONCREST
PUBLISHING

FIRE YOUR FINANCIAL ADVISOR

40 Years of Greed and Exploitation of the American Retiree, and How You Can Fight Back

FIRST EDITION

ISBN   978-1-5445-3817-4 *Hardcover*
       978-1-5445-3815-0 *Paperback*
       978-1-5445-3816-7 *Ebook*
       978-1-5445-3818-1 *Audiobook*

To the overlooked, ignored, exploited, used, taken-for-granted, discredited, unappreciated, discounted primary targets of a financial industry that has taken advantage of you for too long—this book is for you. This book is dedicated to all the 95-percenters.

CONTENTS

DISCLAIMER AND CHEAT SHEET

DISCLAIMER

Now listen.

If you are a financial advisor who has made a career amassing a substantial book of retiree assets and charging a 1% fee for the privilege, this book will definitely not be for you. Prepare to have your feelings hurt.

All you retirees out there who have less than $2.5 million in your retirement accounts, I wrote this book for you.

If you have over $2.5 million, this book *might* not be for you. But hear me out. Even if you are cracking open this book in your first-class seat on your way to the islands, what it says will still make sense to you. It could help you look under a rock you didn't know about, or maybe it could help your parents, grandparents, or the other 95% of retirees (there are almost fifty million of them) who are below that magic $2.5 million mark make it through retirement without losing their life savings.

CHEAT SHEET

Part I—These chapters will show you how and why your retirement dollars got caught in the crosshairs of one of the largest industries in the world—the financial services industry and what that has cost the American retiree. Skip this part if you don't care how we got into this mess in the first place.

Part II—This part of the book explores the new financial guide to retirement in the Information Age. Skip this part if you don't care what new services and person will eventually replace your financial advisor.

Appendix A—If you just want a quick checklist to determine if you should fire your financial advisor, skip the whole book and start here.

Appendix B—If you've already decided you want to fire your financial advisor but need help doing it, skip the whole book and start here.

ABOUT ME

When someone asks me, "Why did you write this book?" it would be easy for me to rattle off, "I hope the reader fires their financial advisor." I really do, but that's not my first answer. Finance books are usually dry, complicated, boring, and overall tough reads. So in truth, I simply hope that whoever opens it—you—will find it interesting, funny, and easy-to-read and enjoyable enough that you will want to keep reading to the end. In short, I wanted to write a book that readers want to finish. That's it.

Now, firing your financial advisor isn't a decision anyone takes lightly—so before we start, you deserve to know something about the guy who's telling you to do it.

Well, I am regularly described as the biggest asshole—with the biggest heart—you will ever meet. Of course, I don't think that is 100% fair, but I guess it isn't my call. I never yell or scream. I don't judge books by their covers. I am a relentless and loyal friend—I do what I say I will do—and I protect the people I love. But I admit that I do speak directly and without apology about what I see in the world, and that unfiltered approach can get me in a little trouble. My response to that is, you don't change the world by getting in line and following.

This book will probably add a few more votes to the "he's an asshole" list, but I don't care. I believe the world needs to change. This story needs to be told because, at this moment in the United States, there are fifty million retirees being overlooked and exploited by the financial industry.

I really care about the 95-percenters who get overlooked because their accounts aren't big enough. I care because their life savings should get the same attention as those of the top 5-percenters. I care because they worked hard their whole lives to get to retirement, maybe even harder than the 5-percenters, but are regularly overlooked by the professional services industry.

Most of all, I care because I was raised by those 95-percenters.

My old man was a factory worker, my mom a schoolteacher, my grandpa a meter man, and my grandma a school bus driver. I was raised in small-town, rural Ohio with a wood-burning stove and no air conditioning. I've got a Stetson hat, a pair of Lucchese boots, a slight Ohio drawl, and the scars from one too many bar fights over the years. By any standard, I'm a certified hillbilly. Growing up, I knew what it was like to be lower-middle, middle, and upper-middle class: never rich, never that poor, always somewhere in the middle. When I entered this world in 1980, my dad was a laid-off construction worker and times were tough. Yet by the time I graduated high school, he had worked his way up to a management position at Honda. I had a basketball hoop outside, wore Nike shoes, and drove a cherry red '89 Jeep Wrangler.

Life was good. My parents showed me and my brother that hard work matters, and proved it by living the American Dream. They raised our social class three rungs over fifteen years of sixty-hour work weeks, with dad on the assembly line while mom was dealing with obnoxious high school students and raising her boys.

Their example stuck. I wanted to keep pushing. No Aler had ever earned a law degree—or any other advanced degree for that matter—so I pressed on through college at Miami University, graduating with a degree in finance and a minor in political analysis. I spent four months in London, England, a crash course on what it really means to be a grown-up working and surviving on your own. Then it was off to law school at Case Western Reserve, where I graduated with honors. Lucky me. It turned out I'd won a one-way ticket to five years of big-law purgatory in Chicago, at one of the largest and most profitable law firms in the world. Following my dad's footsteps logging sixty-hour weeks (on a light week). Pulling regular all-nighters. Dealing with faceless million-dollar clients. And it all boiled down to just billing as many hours as possible each day to make rich people richer. No matter what it paid, it rang empty for me.

Yet that experience changed the man I aspired to be. It woke me up and helped me realize who I was, where I was from, who I wanted to help, and what I wanted to do with the rest of my life.

I wanted to work with, be around, and truly help the 95-percenters. And that meant reinventing what it meant to be an attorney, tearing down the legal industry, and rebuilding it better.

No big deal.

A BETTER SYSTEM

Off to the races I went. At thirty, I resigned from one of the most prestigious law firms on the planet and opened a two-man estate-planning law firm with an old law-school buddy who left his big firm life in Atlanta to come back to Ohio and help me change the world. This was my *Jerry McGuire* moment.

I was convinced that estate planning didn't work because the world had changed and attorneys hadn't. It seemed to me that attorneys were just selling legal documents, and not doing much when it came to helping families navigate life. They were missing the whole purpose of estate planning, which is to help and protect families! They had forgotten that life keeps happening. Health, family, and finances all continue to change even after someone has signed their estate plan, but families never reach back out to their attorneys to get advice on updating their plans because they don't want to be put back on the hourly clock. They don't want to pay $250 to tell their attorney they have a new grandchild or moved to Florida.

The culprit? The billable hour. Most estate plans eventually failed because nobody ever talked to their attorney after they signed their documents. People assumed they were "covered" for everything life could throw at them.

In many cases, they assumed wrong. And sometimes that assumption cost them everything.

I knew we could do better. I knew we could create a better system, geared toward helping everybody and not just the millionaires.

And we did.

We built AlerStallings, a law firm that puts 100% of its focus on setting up legal plans for retirees to help them navigate end-of-life and nursing-home crisis situations. We started by replacing the antiquated billable hour with easy-to-understand, up-front package pricing. Next, we implemented a no-tie policy. Our demographic was already uncomfortable in a law office, and we wanted them to feel welcome. But the most revolutionary change we implemented was that we offered lifetime support (we called it our "Heart"). From the day we opened our doors, any client has been able to call our office with a question or life update and never see a bill. This ensures that their plans work not just when they're signed, but when they're actually needed. We did the impossible. We created a law firm full of attorneys with heart.

Over the years, we've become one of the largest elder-care law practices in Ohio—and the country—with more than 5,000 clients across thirteen offices. This has given me an unparalleled look into the lives, goals, concerns, and *financials* of everyday retirees. And while my big-law stint helped me see how broken and out of touch with everyday retirees the legal industry was, my time at AlerStallings has shown me that the financial industry is worse. Much worse. Big companies have backup dollars to burn, but retirees do not.

So there I was, sitting on my back porch drinking a beer with Tim Stallings, the cofounder of AlerStallings, and we were whining about the unbreakable loyalty our clients showed their financial advisors. Nobody seemed to see what was happening, and if they did, they didn't seem to care. Or perhaps it was just me whining. Anyway, I was frustrated that many of our clients wouldn't move forward with our legal recommendations without first running the decision by their financial advisor.

Seriously—what did we know about legal planning for retirees? We only had a platoon of strategic attorneys with seven years each of higher education and decades of cumulative planning under our belts, all exclusively for this exact scenario and stage of life. Financial advisors, on the other hand, don't even need a college degree to get their securities or insurance licenses. That's right. They don't need any higher education at all to sell investments and handle the management of families' *entire* life savings. It's mind-blowing. Much more on that later.

Back on my porch with Tim and our Budweisers, I felt pissed and helpless. Our legal planning didn't matter at all if our clients ended up losing their life savings by following their financial advisors' investment-centric advice. We were in a losing fight against a trillion-dollar financial services industry.

Tim and I shared stories of clients losing homes and retirement accounts, and other tragic endings when clients relied on their financial advisors alone to face the biggest risks in retirement. Meanwhile, the financial advisors were winning. Their industry had the money and influence to create a narrative around retirement that ensured that nobody was paying attention to the things that really mattered to retirees. Instead, they kept the focus on what made them more money, which was picking and selling investments.

Our law firm couldn't make a difference. Retirees meet with attorneys once or twice throughout the years of their retirement; that couldn't compete with a lifetime of annual meetings with their financial advisors. Retirees couldn't hear us. It was far easier for them to ignore us when it came to their finances and taxes and continue to rely on the financial advisors they had known for twenty years—the same financial advisors who, ironically or not so ironically, never mentioned any of the biggest risks of retirement. The same financial advisors who continued to sell them the same investments during retirement that they had before retirement—as their solution to retirement planning.

A NEW TYPE OF RETIREMENT PLANNER

Then a light bulb went on for me (or maybe it was the porch light). Why did we keep trying to play a game we knew we couldn't win? The finance industry is too big, and it's rigged. So why not stop playing their game and create a new one? I'd created a new type of law firm, with new services and a new type of attorney. Why couldn't I do the same for finance?

What if we created a new type of planner? A planner who only works with retirees coming down retirement mountain. A planner who only works with the hardworking 95-percenters who have less than $2.5 million in assets. A planner who focuses on the real problems of retirement, not just picking and selling investments like most financial advisors.

And that's what we did. When we formed our own financial services company, Golden Reserve, we created the role that had been missing for these same retirees: the Retirement Planner. Our firm's professional services team of attorneys, CPAs, and Retirement Planners works together for retirees, all under one roof.

What a ride. Building two companies over a single decade to disrupt and challenge two of the oldest, largest, richest, and most powerful industries in modern history: the legal field and financial services. Why not? This hillbilly has always been ready for a fight, and I am telling retirees: Wake up, join the fight with me, and fire your financial advisor.

This book is me ringing the bell for the first round.

Over the last decade, people have asked me why I started a law firm and a financial services firm, especially at a time when my beautiful wife, Fernanda, and I were starting a family and then raising our three wonderful rug rats, Lilly and the twins, Lola and Louie. After all, there isn't much calendar space left when you have a family and are running a couple of start-up companies. And the same people ask why I would risk it all again, poking the financial services bear by writing this book to challenge its gravy train.

I always come back to the same answer: my parents. And not just my actual parents, but who they represent, which is the majority of Americans: the enormous but overlooked 95-percenters who are the workhorses of the economy, the unsung heroes. The folks who never make it to a Mercedes but still find a way to send five kids to college. The underdogs. They light my fire and motivate me every morning.

I think of my dad getting up at 4:30 a.m. every day for twenty years to drive to the Honda plant. I think of a story I overheard my mom telling one of her sisters (she was one of nine). She said, with a mother's pride, "I knew we had *made it* when I didn't have to save my spare change in the empty Folgers coffee can on top of the stove to pay for my boys' basketball shoes." My eyes water every time I remember what they gave up for me and my brother. For me, that story is the story of America.

And it's also why I opened both my companies and wrote this book—for people just like my mom and dad.

INTRODUCTION

Fifty years ago, rotary phones took thirty seconds to dial a single number. Antenna TVs had fewer than five channels. Movies could only be watched in a theater. Hubba Bubba even had a soda. And the idea of retirement didn't even exist.

No wonder we're so bad at planning for it.

Around two million people retire every year in the United States.[1] Well done, them. With luck, they'll get to kick back and enjoy their grandkids, go to Florida when it gets cold, and take it easy in their golden years. But it wasn't always this way.

In the Roaring Twenties, around 60% of men who hit the age of sixty-five had to keep working.[2] And at that time, the average life expectancy was a mere fifty-seven.[3] In other words, our grandparents or great-grandparents worked until they died. Back then, on the brink of the Great Depression, families weren't accumulating any savings. They were focused on keeping the heat on in the winter and stale bread with bean soup on the table each night. Wondering which house to rent at the Florida Villages this season wasn't on their to-do list. Simply put, the idea of retirement just didn't exist.

Fast forward almost twenty years to 1940, when Uncle Sam issued the first Social Security check for a whopping $22.54.[4] Wow, thanks, Sammy. Needless to say, that amount of money didn't lead to many folks spending their summers in Europe. This meager attempt by the US government to build a "pension" for aging Americans, so they could clock out a little bit earlier in life, didn't get it done. Almost 50% of men over sixty-five in the 1940s kept working until they died.[5]

There were some marginal improvements in the 1960s and 1970s, but the worker bees still worked and worked and worked until they couldn't work anymore. That generation, our parents and grandparents, lived through the Great Depression and still remember the fear and pain of cold winters and empty stomachs. The United States was still trying to figure things out for the 95-percenters (most of us), so retirement continued to elude the masses.

THE DAWN OF RETIREMENT

Then the 1980s happened. President Ronald Reagan pushed a pro-economy and pro-business agenda, and interest rates finally started to come down from almost 20%. This drove new business opportunities across the United States, with companies like Honda moving manufacturing from Japan to Marysville, Ohio, and the appearance of some of today's corporate giants, including Adobe, Whole Foods, Staples, Costco, and Jimmy John's.

The United States began one of the most spectacular economic runs in the history of the modern world. For perspective, in the twenty years from 1950 to 1970, the Gross Domestic Product (GDP), one of the primary indicators for economic size and health, grew close to 270%.[6] Over the next twenty years, from 1970 to 1990, it grew by almost 500%.[7] The economy was growing twice as fast as before—and it wasn't slowing down.

Why does this matter? I'm glad you asked. It means that, in the 1980s, a majority of Americans started accumulating wealth for the first time in this country's history. Savings and retirement funds were doubling. And that meant that the idea of being able to stop working before you die wasn't just a pipe dream. It was a reality. The dawn of retirement was finally upon us.

That was just forty years ago.

And by the 1990s, things started happening fast. The middle and upper-middle classes had never retired before, so they needed immediate advice. And no one knew what they were doing. Pensions were disappearing. 401(k)s were new. Mutual funds were new. Individual retirement accounts (IRAs) were new. And you know what else was new? Local financial advisors. New retirees needed advice, but there weren't enough advisors to go around. There was a supply chain problem. Everyday folks were no longer part of huge pensions administered by big shots on Wall Street. Instead, the country was full of millions of "Uncle Joes" with $50,000 retirement accounts who had no idea what to do and were in desperate need of immediate financial help.

FINANCIAL ADVISORS VS. RETIREES

To make matters worse, the world continued to change. New

risks were surfacing every year, and planning needs that retirees could no longer ignore—and yet the financial industry dug in and stubbornly refused to adapt to a new world. Why? Money. Financial advisors were (and are) making a ton of it. And despite the industry now having almost a half-century of experience in preparing people for retirement, financial advisors, their services, and their advice have barely changed. Retirees need more than someone picking their favorite investments—but adding new services to support the new needs of retirees is a route in which financial advisors have little interest. Remember, we are talking about trillions of dollars vested in the status quo. So financial advisors stick to the picking investment-only model, because for them it's a winner. And you know who loses? Retirees.

FOUR RISKS

The majority of the fifty million retirees in this country will suffer the consequences of the financial industry failing to address the challenges of today's world. The money they've saved over their working lives is now in danger of being eaten up by the four largest risks that have come to decimate retirement savings but that remain mostly ignored, or dismissed, by an entire industry: (1) the **Tax** liability overlooked on 401(k)/IRA accounts (which really just means when and how much to take out of your taxable retirement accounts, instead of just waiting until you are seventy-two); (2) **Market Risk** adjustments that never happen at retirement; (3) ongoing, hidden advisor and unnecessary investment **Fees**; and (4) the skyrocketing costs of **Long-Term Care**.

That's why this book had to be written.

That's why I'm asking you to fire your financial advisor.

To back that up and better explain how financial advisors have failed retirees, in particular, I use the metaphor of a mountain. Retirement is like Mount Everest. Saving and working for decades is climbing the long way up, which ends in the elation of reaching the summit: retirement. The problem is that *no one* thinks about getting back down and the work it takes to do it safely. Retirees think they are done when they reach the top, the golden years. Yet the way down is much more dangerous, because you have more to lose and no time or job earnings with which to win it back.

You must watch out for the crashing boulders of taxes, market risk, fees, and long-term care, but too many retirees are left alone on the summit by their financial advisors. Or worse, their financial advisors try to get them down by using the same investment-only mentality that got them to the top. That's not going to work. Getting down requires new tools, new services, and new advice.

And a new guide.

That's where the Retirement Planner comes in.

But I don't want to get ahead of myself. Let's take some time for me to build the case for why you should fire your financial advisor. First, I need to show you how financial advisors became the answer for everyone's retirement needs—but the wrong answer.

We're going to start by going back in time. I want to show you how we got into this mess, because the story of the rise of financial advisors—and their imminent fall—is the best explanation of why retirees who want to survive the journey back down retirement mountain need a Retirement Planner, not a financial advisor.

This is no ordinary book about financial planning for your retirement. I'm not going to simply tell you what you need to do; you need to decide for yourself. So if you think you're going to turn the page and start reading about stocks, bonds, and financial planning, think again. We're going to start in a place that was a fixture in most families' lives in the 1980s. We're going to start in the video rental store.

Like I said, this is no ordinary finance book.

PART I

THE RETAIL FINANCIAL ADVISOR

- **9,094 stores**
- **84,300 employees**
- **65,000,000 registered customers**
- **$5,900,000,000 in annual revenue**
- **$800,000,000 in annual late fees**

From $8,400,000,000 to $0, in a little less than thirty years.

That's the Blockbuster story.[8]

The past is another country, they say, and that's true of the 1980s. It is a nostalgic time for many of us. Politics were relatively amicable, technology was changing toys and home entertainment, and the first computers were appearing in homes. Cable television kept adding channels, Sears and Kmart were king, and McDonald's was the only fast-food option in most small towns. Back then, there were travel agents, stores that sold cassette tapes and books, and packed malls full of ladies with those big bangs. Today, those stores and the jobs they provided have disappeared—like cassettes, lawn jarts, and those bangs.

In 1985, a new attraction started to appear in every American city beneath a distinctive blue and yellow logo. It was more than a video store. Walking into Blockbuster on a Friday night was like buying a ticket for an amusement park—but instead of getting on a roller-coaster ride, you took your movie home and buckled up under a blanket on your couch with popcorn and the Reese's Pieces you bought.

It became a highlight of the weekend. You'd meet your neighbors there doing the same thing. You couldn't wait to grab the latest hit: *Back to the Future*, *The Breakfast Club*, or maybe even the latest Bond movie.

Blockbuster was a transformative experience—and it became the undisputed champ of in-home entertainment in the 1990s. It was the largest video store on the planet. The best in-home amusement park in the world (at its peak, Blockbuster actually received approval to build an amusement park in Miami, Florida, but that clearly never happened). It didn't hurt that cable was still trying to figure it out. HBO and other premium channels were just starting to produce original programming. Remember *Dream On*, *Tales from the Crypt*, *Tracey Takes On...*, *Oz*, and *Arliss*? Safe to say, Blockbuster didn't have much competition. Not yet.

They cashed in on their monopoly. A short decade after the first store opened its doors in Dallas, Texas, Blockbuster sold to Viacom for $8.4 billion. Goodness, that is a ton of $1.99 VHS tapes.

But the world started to shift—and so did technology. Top-load Quasar VHS players started to disappear in the late 1990s. Videotapes were replaced by DVDs. Blockbuster lost a bit of their edge—and a bit of their profits. Cable and premium channels were producing popular original hits like *The Sopranos* and *The Wire*; a small company called Netflix started mailing rental DVDs to customers with no late charges; and DirecTV came on the scene. Each of these newcomers took a piece of the in-home entertainment pie that used to belong almost exclusively to Blockbuster. Yet none of those body blows compared to the ultimate uppercut the new world delivered, right to Blockbuster's chin: the Internet. It gave instant access to entertainment and livestreaming. The Internet was Blockbuster's Achilles' heel.

DIGGING IN

Over the early Internet years, the world really started to get away from Blockbuster. Yet they stubbornly dug in and refused to embrace change. In reality, they were simply making too much money to worry about change. And when they did finally notice that the stacks of money were getting smaller and smaller, it was too late. The world had moved on. It was the beginning of the end, indicated by a loss of over half a billion dollars in 2009.[9] The roller-coaster ride was over.

I am guessing that, like other industry giants, Blockbuster told themselves they were too big to fail, that people wouldn't change. Well, that attitude didn't work out so well for Lehman Brothers, and it didn't work out for Blockbuster either. They were delisted from the New York Stock Exchange in 2010 and then filed for bankruptcy. By 2014, the last corporate-owned store had closed. Allegedly, the last video rented from Blockbuster was entitled *This Is the End*. Fitting.

This epic fall from grace as the king of entertainment was shocking. This was a company that had opened only twenty-five years earlier and was worth over $8 billion at its peak. It was like when Mike Tyson got knocked out by Buster Douglas.

No one knew what the hell had happened.

There are a lot of opinions about how a company so successful and powerful rose and fell so quickly. They missed the dawn of technology, the coming of the Internet. They lacked leadership and vision. They were leveraged with too much debt. They were victims of their own success—they were making too much money to change. I believe the most important truth of their downfall was that they didn't have the courage or vision to dream. To be different. And most importantly, to question the status quo.

The inarguable reality is that the world changed. And Blockbuster didn't.

PARALLEL PATHS

So why am I talking about a video rental company in a financial book? It's not as random as it seems. There's another story that feels and sounds eerily similar, and it's the story of the retail financial advisor (RFA). RFAs are your local financial advisors with brick-and-mortar offices on almost every street across America. And coincidentally, the waves of RFAs emerged right around the same time as Blockbuster. Both enjoyed the same unimaginable riches and success over a few decades as they monopolized the entire market, Blockbuster with video rental and RFAs by controlling financial retirement information when there weren't many other options. And they also followed the same path of early success but refused to evolve to meet the changes in the world around them. Blockbuster's path of early success and later stubbornness drove it right off the cliff to bankruptcy.

And just like the home entertainment business, the financial world has seen unprecedented changes over the last forty years. How and when Americans retire now is unrecognizable compared to the past—and so are the support and planning they need in retirement. Despite the changes, however, what RFAs are doing for retirees hasn't changed much. In fact, it hasn't really changed at all.

As I'm going to show you that the financial services industry, specifically RFAs, is going down a path very similar to Block-buster's. Too much money. Too many clients. Too big to fail. Too lucrative to change.

The cautionary Blockbuster saga is being ignored, and history has a painful way of repeating itself when lessons are ignored.

The two parallel stories differ in one very important regard. Blockbuster's unwillingness to evolve cost retirees a nostalgic place where they could grab some candy with a $1.99 DVD, but the financial industry's unwillingness to adapt to the needs of retirees is much costlier.

We aren't talking about DVDs anymore. We are talking about your life savings.

CHAPTER 1

BIG BANG BEGINNING

Penicillin. Plastic. Coca-Cola. The microwave. Rubber. Even Viagra. Each of these world-changing products came from a revolutionary, industry-altering discovery.

We can now add the retail financial advisor (RFA) to the list.

Kaboom. According to the Big Bang Theory (the science, not the TV show), a singularity—one point in space randomly having a multitude of things happen at the same time—created the universe as we know it. What a great accident.

The same can be said every year for careers, sports, and business. The greatest success stories throughout history have combined components of skill, timing, and dumb luck. And sometimes, when all three of those come together, careers are made, championships won, and business empires forged. I am going to show you how arguably the largest and most powerful business empire amassed $26.9 trillion of your retirement money in a remarkably short period of time.[10]

The traditional retirement pension had been the only show in town for almost a century. In the 1950s, 25% of the US workforce expected a pension payment when they hung up the boots and hard hat. That number nearly doubled ten years later when almost 50% of the private sector enjoyed having a pension.[11] The pensions continued to roar until 1978, and the three numbers and one letter changed the financial world forever.

DOMINO 1: THE 401(K) INVASION

Changing the landscape of an entire industry rarely happens due to one shift; it usually takes a number of dominoes falling in sequence. In terms of the retirement-finance industry, the first domino was the Revenue Act of 1978. It added a provision with three numbers and a letter that would forever change the world of retirement: 401(k). Ironically, the intention was not to replace the pension, nor to support employees in retirement, but instead to allow corporations to delay taxes on executive deferred compensation. The 401(k) was brought into being as a benefit for corporations, not employees. Nevertheless, a couple of years later, some clever consultant used this new 401(k) provision to come up with the idea of allowing businesses to put pre-tax money into a retirement plan for their employees while also adding a "company match" component. In 1981, the IRS allowed the funding of these accounts through payroll deductions. Within two short years, nearly 50% of all big US companies had ditched their pricy pensions and added, or were in the process of adding, 401(k) plans.[12]

By 1990, there were nineteen million 401(k) participants. Today there are more than sixty million![13]

It was a game changer. Whereas the defined pension plan used to be the only option for retirees outside Social Security, only 3% of full-time workers had access to a defined benefit plan in 2020.[14] Retirees said goodbye to Wall Street-managed plans and hello to their very own, individually managed retirement plans. But if Wall Street wasn't going to manage those plans, who was?

DOMINO 2: INTEREST RATE CRASHES

The next domino in our Big Bang was the crashing of interest rates. On June 29, 1981, the federal funds rate was 19.83%.[15] I mean, damn. Could you imagine buying a house at that rate? The monthly payment on a $500,000 home on a thirty-year term at 3% interest is around $2,000 each month. At 20% interest, that monthly payment would jump to over $8,000. In other words, the financial environment was tough. It was so tough that borrowing money was not a realistic option for most people—that is, until this domino tumbled.

In the mid-1980s, interest rates came crashing down from 20% to 6%, then to 2% in the 1990s and 1% in the 2000s. And over the last decade or so, the interest rate has been closer to 0%. That's literally "free money."

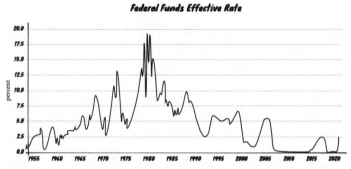

Federal Funds Effective Rate

Federal Reserve Bank of St. Louis, "Federal Funds Effective Rate," Federal Reserve Economic Data, last modified November 1, 2022, https://fred.stlouisfed.org/series/FEDFUNDS.

DOMINO 3: ROARING ECONOMY

And you guessed it. If you give everyone access to cheap money, people will certainly start buying stuff. Add in pro-business policies as pushed by President Ronald Reagan, mix it all together on a large scale, and the economy is bound to respond kindly when people start buying stuff. So, while the Dow Jones was an abysmal 2,461 in July 1982, the interest rate crash was the adrenaline shot the country needed. In a short decade, the Dow tripled in the 1990s (6,000+) and tripled again after 2000 (18,000+).[16] The last twenty years weren't too shabby either, doubling up so that at the time of this writing, it was over 32,000.

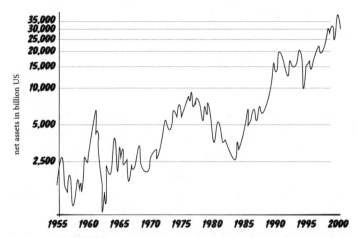

Dow Jones Performance

"Dow Jones—DJIA—100 Year Historical Chart," Macrotrends, last modified November 7, 2022, https://www.macrotrends.net/1319/dow-jones-100-year-historical-chart.

DOMINO 4: BIGGER BANK ACCOUNTS

If that wasn't enough, there was still one more domino to fall: wealth accumulation. In the 1980s and 1990s—for the first time in history—our country had meaningful wealth accumulation across all socioeconomic classes, not just at the top.

These four dominos—401(k)s, interest rates, US economic prosperity, and wealth—were not the only factors, but they were some of the main ingredients that gave birth to the greatest financial services opportunity the world has ever known. And like penicillin, Coca-Cola, and Viagra, it came about by accident.

Overnight, not thousands but tens of millions of American workers started receiving monthly statements for their retirement accounts. And remember, we are talking about the 1980s and early 1990s, when for most people, three television channels, a local newspaper, and, if you were lucky, a knowledgeable neighbor or coworker were the only sources of information about the financial world at your disposal. There wasn't even cable TV.

The change in pensions left millions of everyday people feeling confused and overwhelmed. Retirees needed direction and support on what to do and how to manage these new retirement accounts that had suddenly appeared. Their local newspapers' Sunday financial sections and the local 6:00 p.m. news anchors weren't going to cut it. Everyday Joes couldn't afford the Wall Street boys' advice because their accounts just weren't large enough. Those New York firms had only prime rib on the menu.

America was starving. There had to be another option.

Any economist—hell, anyone who reads more than ten pages of any economics book—would tell you that when consumers have no access to information and no other options, they usually don't get the best deal. In fact, that's putting it too nicely. The consumer gets screwed. That's Economics 101. And that is exactly what has happened to retirees for the last forty years.

Remember, Wall Street was only serving steak that no regular retiree could afford. Now I'll explain how the financial services industry constructed the world's largest and most overpriced hot dog stand in the world.

CHAPTER 2

———

HOT DOG STANDS

Let's start with a question. What did Apple need fifteen of, Subway twenty, and Walmart almost thirty? The answer: *years*. That's the number of years it took for those giants to dominate their respective industries. Building extraordinary things has always taken time. Heck, it took three hundred years (around six lifetimes) to build Notre Dame Cathedral in Paris. Great businesses take time to build, too. Most businesses, that is. What if I told you that the financial industry doubled the size of the mutual fund market in just two years?

Business empires aren't built overnight. They are built over decades of blood, sweat, tears, and more tears. I can attest to that through personal experience, having built statewide legal and financial firms (full of Retirement Planners, not financial advisors) over the last fifteen years. It stinks. It's hard. And it takes time, and a little luck. Almost everyone has endless setbacks, problems, and failures when building a company or industry. That's a fact. And it's just what makes the financial industry's "white squall" explosion into the market so curious.[17]

In Chapter 1, we saw how the financial industry's once-in-a-century white squall moment happened because certain economic and industry-related factors randomly, perfectly came together at the same time: 401(k)s, the interest rate crash, and the US economic boom. Put that together with the realities of the 1980s, when there was no access to information and no other option for retirees, and you get the perfect storm. Americans were starving for financial help. The financial industry knew it—and they knew that people would eat up any hot dogs (investments) they could sell them.

The big problems were that they had no hot dogs ready to sell, and nobody ready to sell them. There were no hot dog stands (investment stores). The financial industry needed to come up with a game plan and blueprint to reroute all these retirees' accounts from the pensions, where they were previously getting paid, to new retirement accounts where they would continue to get paid. The problem was the volume. There were so many more individual accounts to track and service compared to the far smaller number of big pensions they had previously administered.

The financial industry had to dive in quickly, so they got started building their hot dog stands. But their construction plans were delayed right out of the gate by four substantial roadblocks:

1. People—there was nobody to sell hot dogs;
2. Licensure—you had to have licenses to sell hot dogs;
3. Knowledge—the salesmen didn't know anything about hot dogs; and
4. Price—what on earth would they charge for the hot dogs?

Let me tell you how the financial industry pulled off one of the most impressive and profitable pivots of all time. They more or less did a full rebuild of one of the world's largest industries overnight, all while exploiting almost every retiree in the country in the process—and they did it in plain sight, for all of us to see, while being praised along the way by the very retirees whose savings they were pillaging.

THE PEOPLE PROBLEM

The first problem was people. The financial industry had to figure out quickly who was going to sell all the hot dogs to the tidal wave of millions of hungry, working-class retirees. There was a serious supply chain problem. Wall Street didn't want the job. The rich folks had a Smith Barney and a Goldman Sachs, but what most Americans needed was a Kmart.

The industry needed a new role and a new story to tell everyday retirees. They needed advisors who were accessible, trusted, and, most importantly, local—salespeople who could recruit retirees and roll over those new 401(k) accounts with promises of security and growth. And that's exactly what happened. The industry created a new figure, who soon became a staple of every community in the United States: the **retail financial advisor (RFA)**.

Of course, there weren't enough professionals with financial expertise in the country to meet the demand, but the industry needed warm bodies. So the recruitment campaign started rolling, and because nobody really knew anything about finance outside of New York, the industry targeted anyone who could sell. It didn't matter what—cars, cabinets, garage doors, sweepers, appliances, encyclopedias, or even Jesus—if you could sell, you were in. The financial services industry's sales pitch to its new recruits was simple: "If you can sell, we can pay you more. And the folks you are selling to don't really have any other options." It was an attractive prospect for any salesperson. Fish, meet barrel.

Soon, the financial companies were hanging their shingles in every town—large or small, in high-rises, strip malls, and even home offices; it didn't matter. The Big Bang was an explosion of RFAs across the whole country, from Alabama to Wyoming. Their secret was accessibility. Make the RFAs visible. Make them local. Make them someone everybody knows and trusts. That was the key to winning over the 95-percenters. (It also didn't hurt that they controlled all the information and had an absolute monopoly, ensuring that there were no other options available to retirees.)

THE LICENSURE PROBLEM

So now that we had offices filled with warm bodies, the next problem was that these armies of salesmen needed to be licensed to sell investments. How do you license an army of folks who don't know anything about investments? Well, you may not want to hear the answer.

You set the barrier to entry so low that everyone can get a license. And the barrier to handling retirees' life savings entry back then was, sadly, more or less what it remains today.

The RFA needed to be able to sell at least one of the two types of investments:

1. Insurance (annuities, life insurance, etc.) and/or
2. Securities (stocks, bonds, mutual funds, etc.).

And it needed to happen fast. America was hungry.

Let's start with selling insurance. I am a Buckeye, so let's use the Ohio insurance licensing requirements, which are similar to requirements in most states:[18]

1. You must be at least eighteen years old;
2. No additional education after high school is needed;
3. You must complete a twenty-hour, online self-study course;
4. A background check/fingerprints;
5. You have to pay a $42 exam fee and a license application fee, and
6. You must pass an exam.

In less than one month, you can earn a license with zero hours of real-world experience. The only protections assured retirees are that the person taking over the financial fate of their retirement is probably not a felon, paid less than fifty bucks for an exam fee, and passed the exam. Frankly, most people could probably cram and do it all in a couple weeks. And after running that rigorous gauntlet, an RFA can advise retirees and sell them insurance products that control the fate of their life savings. Yup, after one whole month of studying on their own. Do you feel protected?

Shockingly, it isn't much tougher to get a securities license from the Financial Industry Regulatory Authority (FINRA). FINRA issues a range of licenses, so I'll just outline the requirements to sit for one of theses financial exams, a Series 65 license:[19]

1. You must be at least eighteen years old;
2. No additional education after high school is needed;
3. You must purchase a self-study book (literally—it's not even a course);
4. You must pay a $187 application fee; and
5. You must pass an exam.

Once again, without any real-world experience, advanced education, or mentorship, and in just a month or so, you could pass a test and potentially be on your way to managing the security needs of a retiree's IRA accounts. If you're a decent test taker, you could get your license a month after your eighteenth birthday.

This is crazy. Let's think about it for a second. In Ohio, accountants are required to complete a master's program and a rigorous accountancy exam to help retirees fill out even the simplest one-page 1040 tax return. Attorneys are required to complete seven years of school and a difficult bar exam to help retirees fill out a simple, four-page last will and testament.

To be a licensed plumber in the state of Ohio, you are required to:[20]

1. Be at least 18 years old;
2. Have at least five years' plumbing experience/apprenticeship or
    A. Be an Ohio-registered engineer and have worked in the construction or plumbing industry for the last three years (which is basically a four-year degree, so seven years total) or
    B. Have an acceptable amount of other experience as decided by the OCILB;
3. Pay $138 for the exam and $25 for the state license application;
4. Have never been convicted of certain crimes and offenses;
5. Pass the exam; and
6. Carry $500,000 in liability insurance.

So when a retiree calls someone to repair their toilet, the state of Ohio requires any licensed plumber who shows up to have at least five years of real-life experience and half a million in insurance coverage. But when a retiree calls someone to sell them an investment that could make or break their life savings, that RFA only needs to do a month or so of self-study, take an easy exam, and pay a $42 insurance exam fee.

Seriously. This is madness. The regulators in Ohio arguably provide greater protection for our local catfish than they do for retirees (three-year Ohio fishing licenses cost $72.11).[21]

Problem solved. The financial industry made the licensing barrier to entry so nominal that almost anyone could—and still can—join the RFA army to sell investments that could jeopardize the largest asset on every retiree's balance sheet—their life savings. Box checked.

THE PRODUCT PROBLEM

The industry had the RFAs in place, licensed, and ready to sell investments. Now for the final problem. The RFAs lined up behind the hot dog stands, but they still didn't freaking know what they were doing. They had no finance experience. As we've just seen, a high schooler with no experience could be part of the RFA army taking on the trillions of dollars everyday retirees have socked away. So what should the industry do to help all these RFAs who think bond laddering is something you need when repairing shingles on your roof? Who have never even seen a stock ticker? Who couldn't tell you the difference between the NASDAQ, Standard & Poor's, and Dow Jones indices? Newly licensed folks who had never picked a stock in their entire lives were now responsible for making the most important financial decision for millions of families across the country. And unlike much of the merchandise these new RFAs had previously sold (cars, garage doors, and so on), there was no option to purchase a lifetime warranty on the biggest financial decision of their lives: hiring an RFA.

Now the industry really needed an investment tool that was dummy-proof, that even someone who had recently been hired as an RFA could sell to the army of the newly retired. The industry looked into its tool belt and pulled out something that had been around since the 1800s. By today's standards, it is a much-maligned investment option, one that was thought to be dead or on life support after a mass sell-off during the bearish market of the 1960s and 1970s.

The mutual fund.

A mutual fund is often referred to as a fund of funds. That's its genius. It is an investment option that retirees can buy which owns a number of other securities, such as stocks or bonds. This was the *perfect* tool for the RFA. It meant that they really did not need to know *anything* about the financial market, valuations, or performance. They didn't have to pick their own individual stocks and bonds for retirees. Instead, they could simply pick from a dumbed-down list of mutual funds that fit simple risk profiles: high, medium, and low. Then a mutual fund manager on Wall Street—in other words, someone who *did* understand the market—would turn around and pick the stocks or bonds that mutual fund would hold. And, of course, charge the retiree for the service.

Retirees were literally paying their RFAs to pick someone *else* to pick their investments. That created a bigger problem that retirees weren't aware of then, and most are still unaware of today: the double-dip. They are paying double. For every mutual fund they own, the retiree pays their RFA to choose the mutual fund (RFA fee), and then turns around and pays their mutual fund manager again to pick the investments that go into the mutual fund (mutual fund fee).[22]

In the 1990s, mutual funds felt like a brand-new thing. They had no track record, so retirees couldn't check performance or facts (not that there was any place to find this information). And let's be honest, there wasn't really any other place a retiree could go, even if they didn't want a mutual fund.[23] The 1980s and 1990s were a financial black hole, void of options and information— and that hole got filled up with mutual funds, mutual funds, and more mutual funds. To make matters worse, the bull market had begun the epic run that still continues today. People were consistently making more money than ever before, and that did an amazing job of masking, hiding, and justifying the fees being charged by RFAs and mutual fund managers. Although RFAs had absolutely nothing to do with the market's unprecedented success, that sure didn't stop them from taking full credit. Now the masses came to see RFAs as their saviors for retirement, and RFAs dangerously replaced attorneys and accountants as every family's "trusted advisor."

Things were working for the RFAs. Like, really working. The mutual fund industry doubled in size between 1979 and 1981, and it was still only just getting started.[24] Mutual funds became synonymous with market success. Ironically, the indices and underlying equities were concurrently roaring with growth, but that was brushed under the rug by an industry that had hooked the biggest fish they could imagine: the everyday American retiree. Flourishing stocks continued to be replaced with mutual funds, billed as the champion of retirement investing— thus making mutual funds the only real option.

RFAs had found the perfect hot dog to sell retirees.

THE PRICE PROBLEM

People: check.

Licenses: check.

Product: check.

Everything was lined up and ready to go. The last hurdle was figuring out how, when, and what RFAs should charge retirees. On the one hand, as we've seen, RFAs weren't really that qualified; they didn't have to do much work or need to know what the hell they were doing. On the other hand, it was a new business, so there was no real precedent for how retirees would respond or how much they would pay.

Can you imagine the meeting in that dark, mahogany-paneled boardroom circa 1980? I shake my head as I imagine a conversation that went something like this:

Ray: What do you think? We have millions of retirees ready to pay us to sell them investments. What should we charge them?

Ed: [Deep belly laugh] Does it really matter?

Ray: Get serious, Ed. We need to make sure we get ahead of this so those assholes Morgan and Merrill don't get to all this new 401(k) money before us.

Ed: [Ashes his Cohiba, then takes a sip of Johnnie Blue] Ray, stop being such a Boy Scout. The country is full of middle-class mules humping fifty-hour-week jobs to fill up their tiny retirement accounts. They don't know the difference between preferred stock and livestock. Here's what we'll do. We'll charge them twice: once for our advice and again for the investments we sell them. We'll bury our fees in the accounts and investment details, netting them off returns or adding them to losses. The retirees will never know how much, when, or how they are being charged. And so long as we can ride the market and put a few dollars of return in these dummies' pockets, they're not going to care how much we charge.

Ray: Ha, you are so right! I barely understand those mutual

fund prospectus expense ratio calculations and I own a financial company. They will never figure it out. When do we start fishing in this barrel?

Ed: I've already started, Mr. James. One word of advice... stay away from the bigger cities where there is more competition and more available information.

I don't know if a conversation like this ever happened. Your guess is as good as mine. But what I do know is that some variation of it certainly occurred amongst the financial industry's ruling class, with the help of their monstrous lobby and our clueless government officials. Together, they figured out how to maximize screwing working Americans out of their retirement savings.

You see, the financial industry had already seen the tides changing when it came to fees. It had just lost its first gravy train. Before 1975, the primary form of broker payment was getting fixed fees for trading stocks and bonds.[25] It was highly profitable for brokers and highly unfavorable for smaller investors (like me and you) because the size of the trade didn't matter; everyone paid the same fixed price. Then the U.S. Securities and Exchange Commission (SEC) came roaring in on May 1, 1975, better known on Wall Street as "Mayday," which allowed brokerage commissions to set their own rates. The discount brokerage firms were born (you may have heard of the front-runner: Mr. Charles Schwab). Over the next twenty years, transaction fees fell by almost 90%.[26] Unfortunately for the financial industry elites, the business of making money by overcharging everyday people to trade stocks was dead.

The financial industry needed a new and better racket to get money from retiree accounts into their accounts, without anyone knowing.

First, they probably looked at what was already happening. As far back as the 1920s, mutual funds were almost always commission-based products. When a mutual fund was sold, the commission routed to the RFA was called a "load" fee.[27] This fee was usually immediately deducted from the value of the fund sold, so if you purchased a $100 mutual fund with a 5% load fee, your account value would start at $95 after it was purchased. It's hard to believe, but these same load fees have never gone away. They still exist today. You may have heard of A-share, B-share, or even C-share mutual funds? Many retirees think these letters refer to an investment strategy or asset class. Nope. The only thing that letter means is how and when your RFA gets paid their commission for selling that mutual fund: A = up front; B = at the end; or C = over the life of ownership of the mutual fund. And these load fees can be over 5%!

Many well-known financial giants jumped on this opportunity early and rode it hard; not surprisingly, they are still riding it today. Integrity has a price for RFAs—and that price was, and somehow remains, around 5% of the value of every mutual fund sold and then resold regularly (in the industry, the scumbags call it "churning accounts").

Remember, the first generation of retirees were literally financially illiterate. They were an army of new individual investors who had never received an investment statement in their lives... and who had no chance of understanding how the mutual funds they'd just bought would work, perform, or, most importantly, cost.

It was a mess. And it was about to get worse. Leave it to good old Uncle Sam and the soulless financial lobby to give this industry another way to quietly bleed out retirees' saving accounts even more. In 1980, the SEC adopted Rule 12b-1 under the Investment Company Act of 1940. Say what? In short, the new rule allowed additional recurring fees to be charged while you owned your mutual funds—unlike the one-time load commission you already paid up front. This recurring fee can come out of your money every year, forever. So now retirees could get hit out of the gate with a load fee (5% or more) and then the damn mutual fund companies could turn around and pay the RFAs an additional recurring fee capped at another 1% every year.

That's bad, but it gets even worse. The SEC permitted this recurring 12b-1 fee to be netted off mutual funds' gains or added to their losses.[28] This means that no financial statement in the 1980s, or even now, shows retirees the fees they are paying to own their mutual funds. All they see is mutual fund values. Simply put, RFAs have hidden, in mutual funds, how they make money and take money from your retirement account for the last forty years—and they did it with Uncle Sam's help.

HOT DOG-SELLING CONTEST

With all four problems solved, it was now time for the financial industry to attack the retiree market and sell those hot dogs. The RFAs and their industry could charge whatever they wanted. And thanks to this massive and highly profitable propaganda machine being infused with billions and billions of new retiree dollars (and now RFA profit), those hot dogs—not so coincidentally— became the only thing on the menu for most retirees.

The real damage that changed the course of history for retirees was done during the period covered in this chapter, though it might be difficult to see, even now. Despite capitalizing on a strong market and returns, the RFA model was never forced to fight and evolve to meet *all* the needs of retirees in a changing world. Nor has it had an appropriate amount of competition so that its pricing reflects the value of its services. Mostly because of their success, it has been unnecessary for RFAs to think and learn more about everything a retiree is faced with when planning for retirement. Instead, RFAs became an army of salespeople and client relationship masters who did nothing more than sell investments and keep people from asking questions.

That became "retirement planning" in America.

No protection, no real, meaningful planning; just one solution for everything. It was easier, quicker, and—most importantly—more profitable to just keep selling more of their prime rib-priced hot dogs.

CHAPTER 3

—

EVIL EMPIRE

If you added up the 2021 GDP for Japan, Germany, the United Kingdom, India, France, Italy, Canada, and South Korea, the combined total would still be less than the current size of the US mutual fund industry: \$26,964,000,000,000.[29] In 1980, that number was a paltry \$58.4 billion.[30] The US mutual fund market has grown by 46,071% in about forty years.

Weirdly, this growth started at exactly the same time the RFA was born.

What a strange coincidence.

It's not lost on me—this is a lot. It may be a lot to accept that for the last forty years, everyday retirees have been exploited by the multitrillion-dollar evil financial empire and its stormtroopers (RFAs), who focus on just one thing—maximizing how much they can take out of your accounts without you knowing, all while doing the least amount of work possible. And then there's the fact that these stormtroopers probably include your golfing buddy, neighbor, or deacon.

I get it. It reads like clickbait. It sounds like a farfetched claim so this Greg guy can sell more books. It sounds crazy, but it's not, and all I can do to convince you is lay out the timeline of what happened. But I do want to make sure one thing is crystal clear: For retirees, this is one of the two most important chapters in this book. It will show you exactly where you are right now financially. Later, in Part II, we'll look at how you decide where to go from here. Let's jump in.

THE RFA EXPLOSION

Before we dive into the analysis, let me quickly show you the RFA scoreboard and statistics during their rise to absolute world domination and infamy.

In the last chapter, we saw the birth of the RFA. What happened next? Simply put, RFAs dominated the market like Tom Brady dominated football. It's not all that surprising; after all, they created the market, built the market, and then sold the shit out of it. The RFA defined what "retirement planning" meant to retirees. The public was financially illiterate, and the RFA gave them one book to read from and only one: The Holy Book of Investments. And this gospel was preached from every coffee shop by the new RFA in town, who told the masses starving for any information that could "save" their retirement: "Hire me to pick your investments." It's no wonder RFAs multiplied like rabbits, all over the country.

Data and tracking in the early years were sparse, but the RFAs didn't waste much time. They went from being nonexistent, besides a few stock traders and pickers in the big cities in the 1970s, to countrywide domination within a decade.

From the 1990s to the present, the market has been flooded by all sorts of financial professionals fighting to get your money:

- The number of financial services/agents/securities RFAs doubled in the last twenty years.[31]
- The number of personal RFAs went from 77,420 to over 218,000 in the last twenty years, almost threefold growth.[32]
- The number of insurance agent RFAs almost tripled over the last forty years, capping at over one million across the United States.[33]

That is some rapid growth—with a lot of outside professionals joining an industry. But doubling or tripling the size of an industry takes more than just a nice suit, decent hair, and business cards. How could the financial industry support such growth? Well, there was no shortage of retirees with no access to financial information and desperate for advice about their retirement accounts. Controlling access to information and investment options was the RFAs' superpower. And with no Internet, or other investment options, retirees were truly an easy target.

And while RFAs multiplied, so did their favorite tool: the mutual fund. If the financial services industry was the Evil Empire and RFAs were the stormtroopers, then mutual funds were their ultimate tool for retirement-account destruction, their Death Star.

Before 1980, the mutual fund industry was really struggling. There were fewer than five hundred mutual funds in existence. By 1985, thanks to the influx of RFAs, the mutual fund market almost doubled to nine hundred options, growing from $58.4 billion to $218.3 billion.[34] That nearly quadrupled over that same five-year period. It is pretty sad that a financial market could be flooded with an investment that had been around since the 1920s and wasn't good enough for the nation's elite, but was thought more than good enough for the RFAs to push to the unsuspecting middle and upper-middle-class retiree market, who clearly didn't know any better.

Not surprisingly, it is nearly impossible to find meaningful data about the growth of mutual funds between 1985 and 2000. Nor is it surprising that their rapid growth is not celebrated as the savior of either retirement or retirees. Quite the opposite. It feels like it has been quietly erased from the record that actively managed mutual funds continue to be heavily scrutinized. I couldn't find data about the origins of the mutual fund industry on Morningstar.com, or on FINRA or SEC websites built to protect the public. However, I did find some old newspaper clippings. It's almost as if some industries want to erase these numbers from the history books.

From my efforts, I can share with you that from 1985, those five hundred mutual funds valued at $218 billion shot up to around $7 trillion by 2000. And if that wasn't scary or suspicious enough, the number of mutual funds jumped to nine thousand over the next twenty years and were jam-packed with even more of your dollars over the same period, to the tune of almost $27 trillion as of 2021, a tripling in size.[35] I mean, damn. Really? That number is so big it can't be fathomed by the human mind. It can't even fit on my faithful old TI calculator screen.

That is a pretty rich life, right? I mean, that was a Chicago Bulls-like run. But doesn't something seem a little fishy? There was no Michael Jordan. The life of the RFA has been incredibly profitable—but shouldn't we stop and ask why?

Let me pause to talk to all of you skeptics. I know what you are probably thinking: America is growing, wealth is growing, so of course the number of stormtroopers—I mean RFAs—should get bigger. And their biggest weapon—I mean commission, I mean investment tool, I mean mutual funds—should grow, too.

You need more evidence? You got it. You now know that the RFA and mutual fund industry had out-of-this-world growth in a very short period of time, amassing almost $27 trillion (that's $26,964,000,000,000). Well, I'm going to keep shouting from the rooftops that the reason for that was the exploitation of America's working-class retirees by the financial industry as a whole. And now I am going to show you how they did it.

As promised, I am going to dedicate the rest of this chapter to focusing on the *What*. Boy, is there a lot to uncover.

WHAT, WHY, AND HOW

I love telling stories. And I love transforming complicated and technical issues into simple and everyday conversation that is easy to understand. At our law firm, I came up with a campaign called "The Three Big Bad Wolves: Keep Them from Blowing Your House Down." That campaign ran for almost ten years, and was the foundation for building statewide awareness of some of the massive flaws in attorneys' handling of estate planning. It helped normal retirees tackle and plan for the big, complicated topics in what happens after retirement: probate, taxes, and long-term care. Our goal was always related to how we packaged information, never to force a sale—and I believe that's why it always worked so well. We trusted individuals to take the information we packaged and make smart decisions.

Making smart decisions gets more complicated and difficult as the gap widens between the knowledge of a consumer (in this case, you, a retiree) and the market. When it comes to "financial planning," we are talking about a Grand Canyon-sized gap between how RFAs run their businesses and what retirees actually know about their own money. But I am up for the challenge, so let's try to bridge that gap the Evil Empire used to take over the financial-planning world.

Let's break down the *What, Why, and How*.

- *What?* The *What* section, which appears in this chapter, explains what an RFA does and how they get paid, so the two main parts are (1) services and (2) fees.
- *Why?* People often struggle to understand why they should care—or why they should listen. The *Why* section in Chapter 4 shows retirees why not listening hurts their personal finances.
- *How?* This is my absolute favorite. I love the *How*. This section, in Chapter 4, is where I get to explain how such important things as long-term care planning, tax planning, and the

charging of unnecessary fees went overlooked by, or hidden from, the masses for such a long time. You may be feeling skeptical because you never heard about this before, so this part answers the question, "How the hell doesn't anyone know about what RFAs are doing with my money?"

THE WHAT: SERVICES AND FEES

What exactly is really going on with these RFAs and their industry? Let's start with the basics of business. Each business model can be boiled down to just two things: services (or products) and fees. They are the most important parts of any business transaction, whether you're buying a car, choosing an accountant, or hiring someone to plow your driveway. The first thing you do is clearly identify what services are included, and then what you will have to pay. For snowplowing, that might include questions like, "Will this include my sidewalk?" "What about salting?" "What time will you show up?" "How often do you come by?"

Those are just the first questions you would ask to make a decision that could cost you a few hundred dollars each winter. And you know what is pretty wild? Virtually no retiree asks similar questions about the most important financial decision they will make in their lifetime because they don't understand what they are buying. Not the services (or lack thereof). Not the risks to their life savings. And the worst part is, retirees have no idea how, what, or when they will be charged.

Let's look at the services and fees your RFA provides and charges— and why nobody really ever talks about them.

SERVICES

Think about any engagement with any RFA you have had over your lifetime: a meeting with an RFA from Edward Jones, Raymond James, Edelman, Fisher, Thrivent, Merrill Lynch, Morgan Stanley, Ameriprise, whoever. Every first meeting starts off the same, with goals and balance sheets. You think, *Man, this guy/gal is so nice, they listen to me and my spouse, they get us. This feels great.* Then you open up a bit more and share your goals with the RFA, which usually boil down to (1) enjoying retirement and (2) not running out of money. Next, the RFA pivots to their *special* "planning" process. Of course, this is set up to feel customized, thoughtful, and robust—all tailored to your specific goals. There is much talk about Social Security, Medicare, taxes, your insurance, income planning strategies, and estate planning. Man, they are so holistic, they handle everything.

The end of this rainbow comes a few weeks later, when you receive your first statement at home. Despite the multiple meetings and hours of time invested, all you have to show for all that work and meetings is a list of investments and an annual advisory fee contract. If you are lucky, you may even get a special leather financial-planning binder to tuck away next to your birth certificates and passports. Paper-clipped to the inside folder of this binder will be a few business cards of attorneys or CPAs that you are supposed to call, but won't.

Services completed. Now you just sit tight until your next annual review while paying your guy/gal 1% of all your accounts for this retirement "advice." The End.

This is the RFA services package.

That was retirement planning back in 1980. To see all the work RFAs put into developing retirement planning services for the 21st century since then, let's go back over the last forty years and outline the complex evolution of the services offered by the RFA industry:

The RFA's service bundle in 1980—pick investments.

The RFA's service bundle in 1990—pick investments.

The RFA's service bundle in 2000—pick investments.

The RFA's service bundle in 2010—pick investments.

The RFA's service bundle in 2020—pick investments.

The RFA's service bundle *now*—pick investments.

This is hardly groundbreaking, Lewis and Clark stuff. Nothing has changed. The industry started off selling investments as its primary retirement planning service, and currently—oh wait—it still only sells investments as its primary retirement planning service. The only evolution that has occurred is in the way RFAs continue to mask the costs of this investment "advice" and hide it from retirees.

To be completely frank, this is not the way to plan for or protect a retiree's life savings. Evidently it is, however, a great way for the industry to amass trillions of dollars. Don't do much, charge a bunch, and hide how and when they charge. Sit tight—more on their fees in a couple paragraphs.

RFAs' services start and end with what they sell you, and the reason is simple. That is how RFAs get paid, so that is all they do. Even their websites have explicit disclaimers. This is from Cousin Eddie (Edward Jones; the emphasis is mine):

"Edward Jones, *its employees and financial advisors do not provide tax or legal advice*. Clients should review their specific situations with their tax advisor or legal professional for information regarding the tax implications of making a particular investment or taking any other action."[36]

That may seem confusing, and contradictory to what your Edward Jones RFA told you. I know. "Holistic" planners and CFPs (certified financial planners) regularly tout their knowledge and expertise about taxes and estate planning throughout their sales process, but almost every major RFA shop I looked at has a similar disclaimer on their website. This is strange, because most retirees are sold on getting a real, comprehensive plan.

Full disclosure, I don't speak RFA—and you probably don't either. So let me take a shot at a loose translation of what this disclaimer really means in humanspeak:

"I (the RFA) might talk assertively about some important retirement considerations, things like long-term care, taxes, and estate planning. I am going to get fancy three-letter certifications about my knowledge regarding such things. I might even commit these ideas to paper as a 'financial plan.' But all that is really pure sales theater, because in the end I will never build, implement, nor manage or maintain any of the essential retirement tools, such as taxes and estate planning, that I sold you on. This is because I really don't know how and, even if

I did, I still don't have the tools and resources to make them happen. Also, my website says I can't talk about any of this stuff.

But the most important reason why none of these things will ever happen is, I don't get paid to do any vital retirement-planning items. I can only reference them to lure you in and insincerely insinuate my support during my pre-closing sales process. After that, I'll ignore these essential, important parts of your retirement plan. But don't worry. Your 'plan' will end with an investment sale—ideally, a front-loaded mutual fund commission. And then there'll be another full 1% wrapper advisor fee, every year, on 100% of your accounts to pay for my advice—which, though it cannot address any of the risks you will face in retirement, will continue to drive more mutual fund sales.

On an ongoing basis, my services will include birthday calls, a holiday dinner, lunch-and-learns paid for by the companies whose investments I sold you, and, of course, annual review meetings when we talk about your grandkids and I do my best to avoid talking about market performance (when down) or the fees I am charging. Your calls will be returned infrequently when you have genuine questions. I won't work Fridays or weekends. I hope you or your spouse don't have any health issues requiring long-term care, because my plan was to roll the dice with your money and hope that neither of you ever need it. As for my lack of tax planning, I am not worried about it. I will be retired before you see the tax bill on your IRA inherited by your spouse and children. I strategically ignored it, knowing it will be twenty-plus years before Uncle Sam comes knocking to take his 30% or more of your IRA accounts, and by then I will be in Florida. God bless."

FEES

Now that we know what services RFAs do and don't do for retirees, let's look at how they made—and continue to make—so much damn money. It's quite a ride, so buckle up!

The financial industry is making trillions of dollars every year. And all of that money comes from one place: your accounts. That's right. RFAs are very sneaky stormtroopers. You have no idea where they are or what they are doing, but your accounts always seem to be paying for their privilege. And, as with any seasoned assassin, when they pull the trigger on your retirement dollars, you never hear a thing. The money just magically disappears from your account—and reappears in your RFA's account.

For the last forty years, RFAs have been selling investments whose cost nobody knows, and taking their own fees out of the accounts in a way that nobody really understands. Can you think of any other service where you give someone access to your bank account, but have no idea how much they will take out, or when?

Their unlimited access is mind-blowing.

To see just how mind-blowing it is, imagine applying the RFA fee system to grocery shopping. You gather your groceries and go to the register to cash out. But now, instead of the cashier ringing up a total cost and you paying it, the cashier takes away some groceries as payment. They don't ask or explain; they just set items aside as they scan them. You have no idea how much or what was removed, the food just disappears. And even worse, the cashier also has the keys to your home. So without warning, they can come into your pantry every three months, grab your Double

Stuf Oreos, and then go into your fridge to snag your favorite craft beers. No notification. No permission. The cashier takes your groceries. They even take things from *your* house without telling you why or how much, all year long, for as long as you shop at that grocery store. And what they take isn't based on the work the grocery store does for you, just on how expensive your grocery bill was (so if you like the pricier organic stuff, by the way, you're double-screwed).

No other company, business, or industry could get away with such a system. Yet the RFAs and their industry have figured out how to apply it to retirees' largest asset: *your life savings*.

In the last chapter, we saw how, in the 1980s, RFAs used the rules outlined by Uncle Sam and the SEC to help them hide their fees while they charged an up-front load fee on mutual funds and then an ongoing advisor fee. Many of these up-front load charges still exist. One of the largest players, thanks to Cousin Eddie, is American Funds. They have dug in and still charge 5.75% for the luxury of buying their mutual fund: just look at their website.[37] So if you buy one hundred mutual fund shares for $100.00, your account starts off with a $94.25 balance—and then they could slap you with an additional rolling 1% annual fee. (And they charge hardworking Americans these fees, not the 5-percenters, who actually get fee reductions for giving the RFA more money, of course.)

So what does the worst deal ever for retirees mean in dollars for the industry? Let's do some arithmetic.

In 1985, the mutual fund industry was worth around $218.3 billion.[38] Let's be nice and assume a moderate 3% mutual fund commission versus the 5.75% commission I noted above. Apply that 3% against the $218.3 billion mutual fund market and that equals $6.549 billion in up-front load commissions, plus another $2.18 billion in annual, recurring 12b-1 1% fees. Not a bad start—but there are now over $26.96 trillion US mutual fund dollars in the market, so those load commissions could be $808.8 billion, with annual 12b-1 1% fees adding another $269.6 billion. That could give RFAs and mutual fund companies trillions of dollars in fees every year or more. For context, fewer than fifteen out of the 159 countries in the entire world have more than $2 trillion in revenue flowing through their economies in a single year.

Yup, only fifteen countries in the whole world.

Mutual funds no longer just dominate the market. They *are* the market. Mutual funds have gone from the endangered species list, before the RFA boom in the 1980s, to comprising almost 50% of our financial market options. Like Amazon, Walmart, and other industry giants, they are eliminating all other options and controlling the Internet narrative right in front of us—and no one challenges them. They tell you, "Shut up and pay," and you let them. And they can do it because of how much money they are making on almost each and every American.

RFAs have set aside few resources to try and innovate, as the world changes, in order to get ahead of the needs of retirement. Retirees desperately need new ways to provide vital protection to their savings, but instead of new services, the financial industry spent billions of its dollars and resources to create new designations for RFAs and new ways to get paid without drawing too much attention. Unfortunately, none of those fancy Sunday commercials, new letters on business cards, or fiduciary status really do anything at all to help retirees protect their assets.

With any overlooked mass injustice, the truth seems to always find its way out and lead to a reckoning that was long overdue. The Internet was the ultimate messenger of truth in retirement planning, finally providing the masses with the missing information about their mutual funds' hidden costs, fees, and performance woes. The world quickly realized that the actively managed mutual fund world wasn't what it was all cracked up to be. Like cigarettes, actively managed mutual funds are bad for your health, and the word started to spread in the early 2000s. The whispers about the commissions and obnoxious costs grew louder. The information was now out there for all to see, assuming you knew where to look. So the industry needed to create new ways to ensure that their retirement-account-fee faucet kept flowing with trillions of your dollars.

THE FRANTIC FEE-PIVOT

Around 2010, the financial industry and RFAs went back to their original playbook: Target everyday folks, make it complicated, and do everything possible to muddy the waters. And they did it. With a smile. Mission accomplished.

The industry was in a rush to part ways with stock and mutual fund commissions that were quickly falling out of public favor. To make this pivot happen, they needed to substitute investment advisors for mutual fund brokers. Investment advisors have been around since the Registered Investment Company Act of 1940, and are permitted to provide advice and charge a fee so long as they are registered. This is the traditional assets under management (AUM) model, in which the fee for "advice" is a percentage based on the value of the account. Now, that is a fraction of the commission the RFA would've received up front, but unlike load fees, this 1% fee goes on forever.

(Taking the same 1% of a retiree's accounts regardless of size doesn't make sense, by the way; in fact, it defies logic. For any other service, the value of your underlying asset rarely has a meaningful correlation with the work it takes to service it. No one asks how much you paid for your car before they do your oil change. Or what you paid for your house before shoveling your driveway. Or your salary before quoting a knee surgery. Some lawyers may take a percentage, it's true—but only if they win, which assures at least some service-based value alignment. There is no such alignment regarding the value between the consumer and the financial industry.)

Slapping every account from $50,000 to $10 million with the same fee—around 1%—is either mind-blowingly lazy or mind-blowingly greedy or both. An RFA "advisor" servicing anything from a $100,000 to a $2 million IRA is doing more or less the same amount of work from an investment/asset allocation standpoint. I know that every advisor who charges a percentage will be up in arms when they read that, but it is what it is. They are putting on financial theater in the hopes you don't look behind the curtain. And sure, investments may take a bit more strategy from one portfolio to another, but mostly, they involve the same number of meetings each year, the same amount of prep work, and the same overall services (or lack thereof). Yet the RFA earns somewhere between $1,000 to $20,000 for that every year, come rain or shine, based on nothing more than the size of individual accounts.

The kicker? The folks that get price breaks are the folks that arguably need *more* servicing. So the more money you have, the greater the chance your RFA *may* cut you a break and charge 0.9%—in which case, lucky you. Meanwhile, smaller accounts have to pay more in many cases, maybe 1.5%—not because they are getting more services on their account, but because the RFA needs more profit to justify adding them to their fee queue.

What would be fairer, you might ask? Well, how about the same route nearly every other professional service provider on the planet uses: hourly billing or flat fee billing? You work on a case or a job or an account and get paid for that time based on your hourly rate or the cost of that particular service. It's not perfect, but it's simple, and at least there is a real, quantifiable correlation between service and fee. This will never happen, though. It would make too much sense and expose the largest secret of the financial services industry: that they really are not spending much time on their clients. Other than the time they spend trying to acquire their next client, of course.

The key to our story is that RFA brokers living off sale-to-sale mutual fund commissions saw RFA investment advisors living the good life on the AUM 1% gravy train year in and year out. That model meant they didn't have to keep churning (selling mutual funds over and over to the same client) to keep getting commissions every year. They literally just sat back and waited for quarters to end—and their 1% fees just kept rolling in so long as they were investment advisors.

Not to mention, the Obama administration had tried—and ultimately failed—to end those up-front 5+% commissions and ongoing, mysterious, hidden 12b-1 fees, and RFA brokers were now in the crosshairs of the Department of Labor. Lawsuits and bad press brought too much-heightened scrutiny on mutual fund commissions and their ongoing fees.

Now that people could actually see what was happening, the writing was on the wall.

Think rerouting an annual trillion in fees must've taken years? Think again. The RFAs started over and did just what they had been doing since the 1980s. They kept it confusing and, most importantly, they controlled the narrative. They used their media and advertising buying power—paid for by your retiree dollars—to launch a witch hunt against the "terrible" people who took commissions. I know, it's confusing. The RFAs condemning commissions were the same RFAs taking commissions for the previous decade—but don't let the truth or logic get in between an RFA and your retirement dollars.

However, this pivot wasn't just to keep RFAs' pocketbooks full so they could pay those beach house mortgages. The RFAs were also trying to box out a new player: insurance companies. These new insurance companies were making a hefty cut into the RFA retirement market using a new product just for retirees: annuities. The annuity business emerged as the answer to market risk and high advisor and mutual fund costs. It was packaged in a format that was easier to understand and functioned like a better, more tax-preferential version of certificates of deposit (CDs).

The annuity folks went against everything the RFAs had built, so an RFA media blitz made annuities the patsy for commissions, ignoring the inconvenient truth that if you stacked up the commissions from the mutual fund bullies against the commissions from the insurance companies, those mutual fund jerks were ten times the size of the annuity market (though of course, the hidden fee structure with mutual funds meant that there was no smoking gun to implicate *them*, either).[39] Overnight, the market was brainwashed to believe that all annuity commissions represented the "bad" standard. In contrast, the new "fiduciary standard"[40] that RFAs more or less created with the help of the SEC and Uncle Sam to discredit their competition became the new "good" and better standard for retirees.

The new standard, however, has nothing to do with retirement advice, retirement services, years of experience, client testimonials, or anything regarding protecting a retirees' life savings. It only requires that fiduciaries act in the retiree's "best interest." And what the hell is in your best interest? Funny you should ask. Evidently, that's just anything with no commission. And because fiduciaries couldn't charge commissions anymore, RFAs simply started to charge a percentage fee for advice regarding your investments.

That's not a joke. They took the money they were drawing from your accounts through mutual fund commissions and largely replaced it with a 1% AUM wrapper fee on all your accounts for the same privilege.

You know where I stand on the arbitrariness of charging a 1% AUM fee to simply pick mutual funds or stocks for a retiree. Well, this was the world's largest trillion-dollar fee-pivot ever.

Unfortunately, the fee story is not over yet. I saved the worst for last. It's the most shameful and deceitful RFA fee—the one nobody talks about or understands. As the industry took a haircut on front-load commissions, 12b-1 fees, and 1% AUM fees, it needed another way to maximize its returns. (And let us not forget that we've seen how RFAs are magicians when it comes to making dollars disappear from your accounts.)

THE KICKBACK

The RFAs' new trick was one for the ages: revenue sharing. Revenue sharing is evil. Like, Star Wars Emperor evil. The only reason it is not illegal is because our government is either too confused, too lazy, or being paid too well by the financial services lobby to do anything about it.

Revenue sharing is exactly what it sounds like. If an RFA sells a mutual fund or an annuity, the mutual fund pays them a kickback at the end of the year. Companies have been fined by the SEC for hundreds of millions of dollars over the last decade for failing to disclose these revenue-sharing relationships between mutual fund companies and RFAs, and the corresponding kickbacks—but nobody was shut down or went to jail. One of the big ones was the $75 million fine Edward Jones had to pay for failing to disclose such revenue-sharing arrangements.[41] The worst part is that these corporate kickbacks still exist today! And the government has done nothing other than require a library of confusing disclosures that are buried on RFAs' websites.

Kickbacks are almost impossible to monitor because they are set at the corporate level, not at the point of every individual mutual fund sale. A company like Eddie Jones could advertise no kickbacks on certain client accounts but keep kickbacks on other client accounts. How is that possible? Let's say Eddie has a kickback arrangement with American Funds mutual fund company (actually, we don't need to hypothesize; Eddie actually has this arrangement in place).[42] At the end of the year, American Funds cuts a big check back to Cousin Eddie. That is a cost to every human who owns American Funds—no two ways about it. Yet Cousin Eddie advertises that "revenue sharing" doesn't apply to certain account types (the ones paying the annual percentage fee).

I am not buying it. And neither should you. It's a confusing tactic: An RFA can say he won't charge you certain fees, but then sell you investments that charge you fees—and then those investment companies send your fees right back to the RFA. There is no chance that you, or any human, could follow those fees on their ride from your pocket to your RFA's.

My overarching point is that when you charge billions in fees, you control all the levers and can reroute fees so that the only certainty for retirees is where those fees ultimately come out of: their accounts. We didn't even get to the fact that revenue sharing is a blatant conflict of interest. There is an inarguable RFA bias when selling investments that have this kicker. Just look no further than the Wells Fargo PR disaster, when Wells Fargo branches were opening extra bank accounts and services (and charging the related fees) without their clients' knowledge. In a market full of options, which is more likely to be sold to Joe factory-worker: a mutual fund with which the RFA gets a kickback, or a newer fund with lower expenses and a lower commission to the RFA, but better historical performance?

You know the answer. The retiree loses again.

Before I wrap up this fee section, let me just make one thing crystal clear. Despite the bad press and obvious issues with selling front-loaded commission mutual funds with ongoing annual fees, it still happens every second of every day. Actively managed mutual funds are at about the same levels they were twenty years ago—around 7,000 funds remain.[43] Meanwhile, the 1% AUM world grows and grows, because if RFAs aren't making commissions on mutual funds, they are making 1% AUM wrapper fees with juicy kickbacks for revenue sharing.

(Hey, Washington DC! Want a real, meaningful solution that would help every investor in the country and wouldn't cost providers a penny (other than maybe their overpriced fees)? Simply provide two new lines on every RFA statement: one line item for financial advisor fees and a second line item for investment fees (including revenue sharing). Disallow any setoff from managed retirement accounts so these fees are visible, not buried behind gains or added onto losses. Or, if you want to get really crazy, require retirees to cut an annual check to their RFA versus having an automatic deduction netted from their returns. You know, like every other professional service arrangement on the planet.)

If all of this leaves your head spinning, you're not alone. The system is set up as a labyrinth of documentation, disclosures, double-sided statements, prospectuses, hidden fee deductions, confusing expense ratios, kickbacks, and more. How else do you think they continue to get away with making off with a trillion dollars a year in the process?

I get angry and sad writing about fees. The targets were always retirees like my parents and grandparents. The financial companies pulled up a map of the rural areas filled with everyday Americans and began stalking their prey. The worst part is that it was never about helping retirees. It was never about finding the right tools and services to protect life savings.

It always was, and continues to be, about how RFAs with limited financial knowledge can charge retirees as much as they want while doing the least amount of work possible.

How do we continue to fall for the stories, lunches, and dinners? How is it that no one has caught on to these never-ending, unoriginal RFA parlor tricks?

CHAPTER 4

―――

HARRY HOUDINI

The GOAT. Harry Houdini had some tricks up his sleeve. Literally. He swallowed a hundred needles and twenty yards of thread, washed them down with a glass of water, and then pulled each needle, threaded, back out of his throat and across the entire stage. He was buried alive. He pioneered the infamous Chinese Water Torture Cell trick, where he was lowered upside down into a cylinder filled with water while wearing a straitjacket.

Gadgets. Illusions. Misdirection. And a little charm. All a magician's best friend.

How weird that the same items are in the RFA's tool belt, too.

There is no plausible explanation for so many fees disappearing out of millions of retiree accounts other than magic, right? Well, there is, but the timeline and scale at which this RFA theater occurred is the real trick. Retirees were not just ignorant of what was happening right before their eyes; they were cheering the RFAs on all along. They were celebrating a system set up to take advantage of their trust.

Let me show you how they did it, and it's going to be some serious fun—at least for me (not so much for the RFAs out there). I am going to show you the secrets of how RFAs and the industry executed these magic tricks with your money. To do this, we'll circle back to the *Why* and *How*:

- *Why should I care?*
- *How the hell did this happen without anyone noticing?*

THE WHY: RETIREMENT REALITIES

Since 1957 and until 2021, the S&P has averaged around a 10.7% annual average return.[44] That means your IRA has seen some solid growth over the last few decades. If it did, you might be reading about your RFA fees and thinking, *Why should I care?*

It's a good question.

Let's start with some level-setting. Your money has done well—but according to what standard? The market, not your RFA, has been roaring. This means that pretty much every human in the market and a computer can ride index funds cheaply and at a fraction of the cost of an RFA. But I'm not out to waste more time poking fun at the way the smartest financial minds in the world can never consistently beat the indices (although it is one of my favorite pastimes). Instead, I want to make sure we are aligned on the realities of your retirement. I am sharing these *market* realities so you think about what you received in the last five or ten years from your RFA versus what the market itself returned, how much you paid for those RFA services, and what that means for your life savings and retirement.

There are four answers to the question, "Why should I care?" Ready to jump in? Plug your nose. It's cannonball time.

YOU'RE DONE MAKING MONEY

The first answer is easy. You're done working, which means you are done making money. That mindset is a huge shift, not only in terms of your daily routine and vacation schedule but also with your retirement accounts. Most of you are not lucky enough to have a pension anymore, so the very real reality is that no more money is getting added to your retirement accounts. If you needed to pay for something in the past, you could always work harder or longer. Not anymore.

Now you need whatever money you have saved to last so you can enjoy the golden retirement years. Every one of your dollars should matter. The RFA's sole job should be to protect those hard-earned retirement dollars as viciously as necessary, not put them on the blackjack table.

IT'S YOUR MONEY

The second answer to the question may seem strange, but it needs to be said: You should care because this is *your* money. Not the RFA's.

For some reason, retirees have a strange relationship with the money they socked away for decades. Your name is on the account. You can take money out whenever you want, but you feel guilty doing it. These savings have been inaccessible for so long that maybe spending it takes some getting used to.

This "retirement account guilt" happens to almost every retiree. In response, you often just unthinkingly hand the keys to your account over to your RFA. When you worked, you filled up your account—but now you let your RFA make the rules: what you can take out, what you should invest in, what other professionals you should listen to. It's your very own version of Stockholm Syndrome. And the RFAs know it, which is why they treat your account like it's their money.

If you don't believe me, just try making an unannounced withdrawal or switching RFAs. The sirens will go off at your RFA office like someone just broke into their private vault.

THE TIME VALUE OF MONEY

There's a third reason why you should care: the time value of money. The compounding nature of money is hard for the human mind to grasp, because we are terrible at thinking long-term. Our minds are focused on NOW. But the numbers are staggering if you plug them into a financial calculator. If you have around $500,000 in retirement investments and are paying roughly $12,000 in fees each year, that may not seem like a big deal. If you make money, the fees are netted off your gains, so you don't really feel much of the pain. If you lose money in the market, then the fees are added to those losses, so you don't really notice them either.

But what if you didn't pay your $1,000 advisor fee every month? What if you knocked the RFA leech off of your retirement and instead took that money and put it into a separate account with a modest return of, say, 4%? How much money would you have to spend or pass on to your grandkids then? Over ten years: $147,250. Over twenty: $366,776. Over a full retirement of, say, forty years: $1,181,966—all from turning off the RFA annual fees coming out of your account.

That's the power of compounding. *You added one million dollars to your net worth.*

That could be multigenerational family vacations to Hawaii, paying off kids' mortgages, or an entire generation of grand-kids' college tuition—but instead it went to your RFA's summer lake house mortgage payments. RFA fees are very real, and they add up.

YOUR MONEY ISN'T PROTECTED

The fourth and last reason you should care about fees is not just about what you could be saving or making, but about what you could be losing. We will focus on the four risks of retirement more in Part II of this book, but I want to emphasize here too that avoiding or ignoring these risks could cost you everything (and your RFA nothing). Missteps in retirement planning are grave, dangerous, and, worst of all, unforgiving. If it goes wrong, you don't have time to make more money or, in many cases, to get back to even. While it takes days to lose it, it could take years to get it back—and this is the money you need to live on during your retirement years.[45]

That is the biggest reason why you should care. You should do whatever you can to protect your life savings, and if you choose an RFA who uses the same strategy that got you to retirement once you're *in* your retirement, there is pretty good chance that one or all four of those big retirement risks could end up costing you in mere months, weeks, or even days what it took a lifetime to save.

THE HOW: HOW DID THIS GET MISSED?

How did retirees get into this terrible position? How is it that nobody talks about this, or pushes back? How are there not more options? How is this legal? How did your RFA pull it off?

Gosh darn, is Greg making all of this up?

This is my favorite part: I get to show you how an industry continues to pull off their most famous magic trick. And that it really isn't magic at all.

To start, it's important to understand how you think and feel about your RFA. And while we know feelings aren't real, we also know feelings are simultaneously some of the most important driving motivators in our lives. Let me share a story that drives this point right home.

We were working on a legal and financial case, trying to bring on a new client who was working with Edward Jones. It was easily one of the most egregious illustrations of what an RFA could do to a retiree's life savings. The retiree had around $1.5 million in A-share mutual funds and $183,000 in a variable annuity. That's basically the worst of the worst when it comes to investment costs.

The mutual funds had been staggered so as to break them up over three fund families, ensuring maximum compensation breakpoints to the RFA. The up-front charges were over $28,000 (over 5%). The annual recurring costs were another $24,000 (1.64%), plus $3,430 (1.87%) for variable annuity costs. In their first year of ownership, the retired couple paid around $55,000 in fees and other costs to work with an RFA. For one year. The worst part was that they were being pushed to transfer to the "advisory model," which was fairly new at the time.

That would commit them to pay an additional 1% a year on all these accounts—around $15,000—forever.

It was so ridiculous, a partner from one of our Ohio offices called me to ask if we should report this RFA to someone. I remember looking at him and saying, "For what? Unfortunately, somehow, this is legal." We both were excited to help, though. Not only was the fee gouge eye-popping, but we also had a personal relationship with the retired couple. Our own fees and investment costs would have been less than $4,000 a year for all of our services, saving them over $20,000 a year in fees. But in the end, we lost the case. Why? Because the RFA was a "friend" they vacationed with and they didn't want to make it weird.

You really couldn't make this shit up—$55,000+ in fees in one year didn't even matter—and cases just like this still happen every day.

This story epitomizes how the common sense we apply to every other facet of our financial lives is seldom applied to our treatment and view of RFAs. It's emotional and personal, and it defies the logic we apply to all other personal purchases.

Let's look at how I think we got here.

FOUR REASONS

It would probably require another book—and a team of psychologists—to get to the bottom of how other 95-percenters goggle and goo over their RFAs. RFAs' exploitation of retirees has happened again and again, right under our noses. Maybe the easiest explanation is a quote from one of my favorite fictional characters, Sherlock Holmes: "The world is full of obvious things which nobody by any chance ever observes."[46]

There are four big reasons why this broken system has gone

unchecked for so long: (1) countrywide financial illiteracy; (2) a big ol' monopoly; (3) the craziness of groups; and (4) US prosperity.

FINANCIAL ILLITERACY

Let's start off with the average retiree's financial literacy, or lack thereof. Below are a couple of statistics regarding literacy to illustrate my point perfectly:

"Two out of three students who cannot read proficiently by the end of 4th grade will end up in jail or on welfare. Over 70% of America's inmates cannot read above a 4th-grade level."[47]

If you are incapable of understanding the complexities of life, it will be more difficult to navigate it, and harder to make informed, good decisions and avoid bad ones. The same holds true when it comes to your finances.

I have seen how most retirees "read at below a fourth-grade level" when it comes to their finances—things like breaking down mutual fund prospectuses, valuing equities, or navigating the complexities of the IRS tax code. Or knowing what a mutual fund or annuity is, or how they work. Without a baseline understanding of financial terminology and strategy, it becomes highly improbable that you will make good financial choices—which is why you are a walking target for the wolves of the RFA industry.

The 1980s and 1990s were a knowledge blackout, when information was controlled by few and inaccessible to many. The blindfold was tied tightly around retirees' heads for a long time—and their neighbors, friends, and families were all wearing them, too.

Even once the blindfold was lifted, navigating the world of finances wasn't like picking out groceries or a new car. Financial stuff is complicated, confusing, erratic, inconsistent, and overwhelming, even for those of us who are experts—like the complexities of compounding interest, or the mid- and long-term effects of market losses. Most of our minds are not built to process such large numbers, long time frames, or financially complicated concepts. In his book *The Psychology of Money*, Morgan Housel does a great job of breaking down how terrible most of us are at understanding how money and wealth actually work. The book illustrates how our minds struggle to process financial realities over prolonged periods. Housel starts a chapter titled "Confounding Compounding" with, "$81.5 billion of Warren Buffet's $84.5 billion net worth came after his 65th birthday. Our minds are not built to handle such absurdities."[48]

It's true. We simply can't connect the dots. In the past, experts spent a lifetime learning how to navigate the market, financial products, compounding interest, returns, losses, fees, and taxes. Then, overnight, an entire retiring generation was expected to navigate all of it—everything we have discussed—on their own, with no instruction booklet or CliffsNotes on how to protect their life savings. Poor retirees—it hardly seems fair.

How can you change your own financial story if you can't read the first chapter?

MONOPOLY (NOT THE BOARD GAME)

Some companies land on Boardwalk and others on Baltic Avenue. That is business, and life. We've seen how, for decades, there was only one (mutual fund-selling) hot dog stand for retirees.

Why? There were no other options, so the RFA industry was able to provide whatever services they chose for whatever fees they decided.

The RFA industry shaped and defined "planning" and eliminated any alternatives through its power, money, and influence. With that kind of monopoly, it was pretty easy to keep the public lined up and waiting for their next hot dog. And, thanks to the confusing topic and limited access to information, it was also a great way to ensure that nobody asked any questions.

This is no different than the only real operating system available for the last forty years, Microsoft Office. I know, you may have played Oregon Trail on an Apple computer in elementary school. But when it came to business, there weren't any other options outside maybe Lotus Notes. Yikes. Even today, Microsoft is king by sheer size of market, representing over three-quarters of Fortune 500 companies and even a higher percentage of small businesses. Folks may recently have started to explore converting to a Mac operating system, but the reality is that we still are beholden to never-ending updates, clunky features and the limiting of any meaningful innovation until Bill feels like it. That is the biggest problem with only buying one type of hot dog for so long. Whether it be with Microsoft or RFAs' mutual funds, the consumer loses all leverage because there is no competition. This leads to shittier service and products, and again to getting screwed on pricing because there are no other options. Economics 101.

GROUPTHINK

Next up, groups. Groupthink is very real—and pretty terrifying. Individuals can be intelligent, thoughtful, reasonable, and, at times, even rational. Groups, in contrast, are often erratic, unpredictable, emotional, and downright crazy. I encourage you to read Charles MacKay's classic, *Extraordinary Popular Delusions and the Madness of Crowds*.[49] Every chapter is dedicated to a story of how groups of reasonable individuals do strange or flat-out crazy and illogical things—including witch hunts, crusades, and fortune telling. Things go sideways when individuals stop thinking and just follow a group. My favorite is Tulipomania, that craze during the Dutch empire where people traded their homes for certain tulip bulbs before the market crashed and tulips became just pretty flowers again. You don't usually make the best decisions when unthinkingly following a crowd. At least, not for long.

For more evidence of the influence groups can have over us, I don't have to look any further than my own career path. When I was working at one of the largest law firms in the world, I regularly canceled vacations, spent more than twenty-four consecutive hours at my desk, and slept with my Blackberry on my chest. When your bubble of human interaction is only coworkers who are also spending sixty-plus hours a week doing, saying, and acting in the same fashion, your mind can normalize behavior that is not normal. Monkey see, monkey do. Our lives are largely shaped by what everyone else around us is doing.

This sheep mentality is what allowed the wolves to come in. Everyone was doing the same thing, so it was okay. Everyone was exclusively buying investments and using the local RFA on the corner, so it was okay. Everyone was getting charged the same way, so it was okay. Groupthink was one of the largest contributors to the success of the RFAs. Not only was their exploitation of retirees accepted—it was celebrated by the mob.

And now, the fourth reason for how the RFA industry got away with what it was doing: American prosperity. As we've seen already, the economy was—and remains—rolling, so the market was growing at unprecedented rates. People were making money. It was an exciting time. And instead of the credit going where it belonged—to the red-white-and-blue American workers whose blood, sweat, and tears were finally yielding the returns they deserved—it was hijacked and rerouted to the RFA salesman. RFAs were championed as the secret to investment success, and, ultimately, retirement-planning success—even though, in reality, any financially literate adult who put money into any of the indices over the last forty years would have gained the same, if not better, returns.

It is hard to question a system when you have been indoctrinated to believe that your returns, life savings, and retirement-planning success are all thanks to the guy who has been selling you mutual funds and buying you breakfast on your birthday for the last decade. That is a bridge too far for retirees to realize, let alone accept.

The RFAs knew it, so they kept on charging.

This chapter was probably a lot to absorb, but that's the full story of how the RFA industry took over, controlled, and dominated a market. The full magic show. And they did it all while riding on the backs of American retirees, including you.

The longer a magic show goes on, though, the harder it is to keep all the balls in the air and the viewers distracted. Eventually, someone will see the pigeon head peeking out of the jacket.

I promise this book isn't all doom and gloom. Other options and answers are emerging from the darkness of this financial Evil Empire. But before we switch gears and get to the hero of my story, I need to warn you about the scariest and most dangerous villain of them all...

CHAPTER 5

THE VILLAIN

Petters, Stanford, Kerviel, Ebbers... You might recognize the names. They're Hall of Fame villains of the financial industry who amassed millions from unknowing victims and then paid the price by serving hundreds of years of jail time. The most infamous? Mr. Bernie Madoff, who stole $65 billion over four decades and landed a 150-year sentence. Pushing the limits—and greed—drove these villains over the legal line.

Now, what if I told you that the RFA industry can actually erase the line between legality and illegality? And that a Mr. Edward D. Jones might just hold the world's largest eraser?

The last couple of chapters looked at the *what, why,* and *how* of the RFA industry. Now let's spend a little time on the *who.* The industry is packed with companies and individuals who work the system: the charming, smooth-talking RFAs who get you to order up investments with the same ease with which you put in your morning drive-thru coffee order. This RFA might be your neighbor, high school (or worse, peewee) football coach, a fellow Rotarian, a lector at church, a smiling face at the local pub, or even a family member. They certainly will have an office with a big sign on your local main-street corner, and you might even see their commercials on Sunday during the ball game. That is their secret. They hide in plain sight as they build their fortunes by strategically, methodically bleeding dry the accounts of unknowing retirees.

By any measure, one RFA certainly stands alone as a world-class financial mastermind who would even make Bernie blush. Meet the grandmaster of working the RFA fee system, Edward David Jones.

EDDIE'S HISTORY

Before we go down this road, let me share a pretty wild fact I found while researching this chapter. I still can't believe it. I was raised in a very small town—Bellefontaine, Ohio—with a population of less than 13,000. Are you ready for this? The real Edward Jones and I both graduated from the same small Ohio town, Bellefontaine High School.

Unbelievable. I guess you could say that, despite starting in the same place, our lives' missions went in two completely different directions.

How did Eddie and his crew grow to the point that they were able to suck down $12.3 billion in revenue in 2021?[50] The answer is pretty simple. They mastered the art of selling overpriced mutual funds without anyone either understanding or paying attention.

KEEP ON SELLING HOT DOGS

Edward Jones is the David Copperfield of RFAs, but instead of making bunnies disappear, Eddie vanishes retirement dollars to the thundering applause of the retiree crowd as they cheer him on to another billion-dollar fiscal quarter. To quote Verbal in *The Usual Suspects*, "The greatest trick the Devil ever pulled was convincing the world he didn't exist." That is Cousin Eddie's secret sauce. He does it all out in the open, in plain sight, for the world to see. That is the real genius behind his villainy.

Cousin Eddie started down this dark road a long time ago. To maximize his fees and maintain his advantage over middle-class Midwesterners, Eddie partnered with mutual fund companies early in the game, companies like American Funds and Black Rock. They set the gold standard for pushing fee limits, charging up-front load fees (5% or more) while receiving ongoing 12b-1 fees every year (around 1%) that are buried in your quarterly statements in an undefined category of annual "planning fees," and that provided their rocket fuel. They can churn the account whenever appropriate, using a market uptick or downtick as a reason to "rebalance"—and get paid all over again. They may even charge an "exit fee" to get out of the investments they sold you if you choose to leave your Edward Jones RFA.

KICKBACK KING

The revenue-sharing thing (i.e., the kickbacks they got from mutual fund companies) got Eddie in a little hot water over the years. Don't believe me? Just ask the SEC. They slapped Eddie on the wrist with a $75 million settlement in 2004 for, among other things, receiving $82.4 million in undisclosed payments (i.e., kickbacks) from certain preferred providers.[51] That accounted for almost all of Edward Jones' mutual fund sales. In other words, Eddie sold a bunch of mutual funds, and the mutual fund companies gave them back almost $100 million of those sales in the form of revenue-sharing fees. That, ladies and gentlemen, would be quite an incentive for your local RFAs to push one mutual fund product over the others, right?

The problem was that Eddie didn't tell their clients about this $100 million arrangement. Oops.

THE DEPARTMENT OF LABOR

Instead of shutting them down, the Department of Labor just hit them with a fine. I know it sounds like a lot—$75 million to avoid criminal charges from the Justice Department. But for some context, a $75 million fine to a billion-dollar company is like a high school teacher who makes $75,000 a year having to pay a $5,000 fine because they screwed up their property taxes. That's the price of a family vacation to Florida. Worse still, the go-forward solution was *not* to make revenue sharing *illegal*. Instead, Eddie simply had to add another disclosure to their advisory documents and to their website. Yeah, that should do it, since everyone always reads the fine print.

For fun, search the phrase "Edward Jones Revenue Sharing Disclosure." Then try to navigate the dozens of disclosures on their website. If you are lucky enough to find any mention of revenue sharing, good luck trying to make any sense of it. I was a contract attorney for a decade, and I had to read it three times to even start to understand what they were saying.

Confusing word jumbles are the only protection millions of retirees have against these kickbacks: word-puzzles buried in a stack of other word-puzzles, on a piece of paper covered in tiny print. Geez, thanks, Uncle Sam.

MORE LEGAL PROBLEMS

The lawsuits kept on rolling in. In 2006, Eddie Jones settled another class action suit. This time, it was a fine of $127 million for undisclosed kickbacks to mutual fund companies.[52] Again, there was no Department of Justice involvement, and there were no criminal charges or real changes to revenue-sharing rules. Retirees remained ignorant and an easy target. The financial lobbyists in DC did their job positioning meaningless change... and retirees lost to the RFAs. Again.

Last but not least was the class action lawsuit filed around 2018 that accused Cousin Eddie of "reverse churning." This allegation was based on them frantically pushing clients into their percentage "advisory solution" model accounts, which can charge over 1% annually. Ironically, that was their attempt to leave behind the bad press associated with their usual mutual fund sales and revenue-sharing model (kickbacks). And Cousin Eddie and his RFAs justified this—brilliantly, I might add—under the guise of the Department of Labor changes. I'm guessing their pitch went something like, "Uncle Sam is making me charge you 1%, so let's sign you up for the advisory solutions model." Clever, but in my opinion, this was all a lie to get out of mutual fund commissions and into the 1% fee-world as quickly as possible.

Regardless, the complaint stated that "advisory solutions" retirement account values jumped from $101 billion in 2013 to $265 billion by 2017.[53] As of mid-2022, it's unclear where this case stands after a California judge dismissed it in 2019, mainly because—wait for it—Eddie did provide disclosures to clients this time around. (Disclosures, by the way, that we can all agree almost no human of even above-average intelligence could ever understand.)

This last lawsuit and its numbers are certainly the most compelling example of Eddie's treachery, as it aligns perfectly with the fee story I told in the last chapter. Having been fined roughly a quarter of a billion dollars, and with the tide turning as people started to understand that paying 5% for an A-share mutual fund plus ongoing RFA fees wasn't that much different than stealing, Cousin Eddie had to change course before the revenue dried up—and do it quickly, while holding a smoking mutual fund gun. They pushed the hard pivot button to go the way of the newly popular wrapper 1% AUM model, but they pushed their client conversion pace so hard that they got hit with another class action suit. This time, though, it was too confusing for even the courts to follow.

Edward Jones allegedly moved almost $200 billion from one RFA model of screwing retirees to a newer RFA model of screwing retirees—only this new model was arguably even more sinister for all those clients who transitioned (often without understanding why). You see, those clients had already paid the mutual fund commissions and ongoing costs under the promise of years of performance without any additional cost. However, they were now promised new and better "advice" in exchange for a *new* fee without getting the value of the cost they had already paid the first time around. The problem: the fees they paid the first time were not credited or washed away. Instead, they had the pleasure of being immediately charged not just 1%, but the new 1.35% annual advisory fee.[54] Quite the double-dip, and the government and courts appeared to have given in.

Cousin Eddie did the impossible and slipped the hangman's noose—again. At least for the time being.

Don't get me wrong: Plenty of other RFAs mirror Cousin Eddie's moves, albeit on a less grandiose scale and without pushing the absolute breaking-point limits of how much can regularly be pulled from a client's account in fees before the Department of Labor steps in. But most RFAs have a similar philosophical approach; they talk about investments and how they charge, *not* about what services they provide to help retirees. Shockingly, many RFAs still sell the original front-loaded American Funds mutual funds that made Eddie rich and are now regularly blasted by the media, the government, and me, every day.[55]

PICKING ON THE LITTLE GUYS AND GALS

All these slimy moves, lawsuits and bad press have to be enough to clinch the RFA bad guys' gold medal for Cousin Eddie—but there is more. It wasn't just how they continue to charge, charge, and charge again. Their plan remains even more calculating and despicable.

It was *who* they targeted. They didn't bother with the bigger accounts. From what I can tell, they dove into towns with fewer than 50,000 folks and targeted smaller accounts (with their meager $5,000 minimum account size requirement).[56] I believe they were searching for lower levels of financial awareness along with lower levels of competition. Then built brick and mortar across Middle America and pushed forward to get as much blood out of every retiree turnip as possible. They targeted all you 95-percenters and bullied their way to billions.

Proof?

My firm has an office in Lima, Ohio, which has a population of roughly 40,000. And if you ask the Internet, they have had twelve different Edward Jones offices pop up as of July 2022. But look up Columbus, Ohio, the state capital, with over a million people and counting. How many Edward Jones offices appear at the same time? Nineteen is the number that popped up on my screen. With a population twenty-five times the size of Lima, you would expect the number of Cousin Eddie offices in Columbus to be commensurate, around 300 (25 × 12). But nope. It's just nineteen in the whole city. And it's not a coincidence.

According to *Magnify Money*, only 12% of all Cousin Eddie investors have more than $750,000 under management or a net worth of at least $1.5 million.[57] This is because Eddie set out to target the backbone of America: the middle class. Successful RFAs are the ultimate relationship masterminds. They have the recipe for how to infiltrate local communities at Mach speed. They join churches, rotaries, school boards, charities, and Kiwanis, and will greet you with a wave and a smile every time you see them walking down the sidewalk or grabbing a local coffee. They know that if they get to feeling like a "friend," almost no one will ask questions.

Middle-Americans outside the bigger cities trust their neighbors more. That's a fact. We didn't even regularly lock our doors growing up. It is just who we are, and how we were raised. Eddie knows this better than anyone. Calling you about your kids, inviting you to a happy hour or birthday dinner, maybe even taking you on vacations—RFAs will do anything to click the handcuffs and pull off the ultimate retirement-account heist, preying on Middle America's trust and vulnerability all the while.

I challenge anyone reading this book who chose their RFA solely on the strength of their relationship, not their services, to ask themselves one question:

"If I took my business away from my RFA, would they still call me on my birthday and be my friend?"

We all know the answer. And we all know friendship shouldn't come with a quarterly statement.

We started this chapter talking about some folks who crossed the criminal line—but exactly where does the line start and end for RFAs? It is hard for me to figure that out, even as an attorney, so I'm guessing it's even harder for most retirees.

The definition of criminal fraud is "a crime that involves a scheme to cheat or deceive another individual or entity in order to obtain a financial gain or similar type of gain."[58] Well, throughout the first half of this book, I've outlined the lengths to which the RFA industry has gone to disguise, hide, confuse, and bury the different ways they take money out of *your* account—and move it to their own. RFAs have been able to confuse retirees and manipulate their retirement accounts for the last forty years. How is that anything other than "a scheme to cheat another individual or entity in or to obtain financial gain"?

Maybe it is the sheer size and scale of the industry that enables it to pull this off. If everyone's doing it, can it really be wrong? I guess we'll have to wait on the Department of Labor or the Justice Department to have the courage to stop looking the other way and act on the continuing exploitation of working-class retirees by the financial services industry across the country, decade after decade. Or maybe the retirees will finally band together and push back—push back against the status quo of exploitation by an industry that has left them alone and unprepared for the trials and tribulations of surviving the new risks of retirement. Only time will tell.

As for Cousin Eddie, they sure aren't slowing down—and I'm guessing the executives in St. Louis are sleeping like babies every night. As the number of advisory accounts continues to soar, Eddie's transition plan is working. You see, you can't go from $5 billion to becoming a $12.3 billion Goliath in less than ten years without knowing how to bend, move, or erase that line I keep talking about, that line that establishes legal or illegal, good or bad, right or wrong.

Ask around—I assure you that I am no altruist. And I don't hate companies that make buckets of money, either. I understand that success and growth come at a cost. But at what cost?

Well, Edward David Jones certainly did the math, and figured out how much they were willing to take and pay to get their billions. It was no more than a few hundred million in fines every few years and, of course, their integrity.

Sadly, retirees continue to gravitate to the familiar. They assume it's the only option to let RFAs use their accounts like their own personal piggy banks. They don't question the system, or their RFA.

You might be thinking, *Well, it's fine for this Greg guy to keep railing against the machine, the Evil Empire. He's got me pretty pissed about the unfairness of it all, but what's the alternative?*

I'm glad you asked. In the next part of this book, I'm going to show you. And I promise, it's going to come as a very welcome surprise. The retiree finally gets to fight back. All it will take is changing the entire financial framework, fees, philosophy, and system. But don't worry, I have some ideas, and might already have gotten started on that.

So get your rocks and sling ready. We're going after Goliath!

PART II

THE RETIREMENT PLANNER

Here's another story in numbers:

- 15% of the Internet's bandwidth
- Over 200 million subscribers worldwide
- Over 70 million US & Canadian subscribers (almost one-third of the adult population)
- From $0 to over $25,000,000,000 in a little less than twenty-five years

That's the Netflix story.[59]

The way we consume information has shaped civilizations since the dawn of humankind. Theater and the Roman Colosseum, sports, newspapers, and radio: over the centuries, they have been ways to occupy, distract, and entertain the masses. Around the start of the 20th century, a world-changing package combined visual and audio recordings in the United States' first movie theater, the Nickelodeon.[60] The public was 100% sold, and Hollywood in Los Angeles soon became the world hub of the movie business. Soon, US innovation meant that everyone could have their very own movie screen at home, as TVs grew in popularity until they became virtually mandatory by the 1950s.

The next advance took a little time, but around the 1980s, the VCR boom began, bringing the joy of the movie theater to your living room. About a decade later, the experience became even more convenient, and the quality of the viewing experience better, with the DVD. In less than a century, the world brought the kind of entertainment people had enjoyed for thousands of years in the Colosseum or the theater into the home.

That is where I want to start the next part of my story.

Let's hop back in that time machine again. But instead of going back to the 1980s, let's make a more recent stop—in 1997, to be exact. Floral anything and Dr. Martens were in fashion. Foo Fighters were on the radio. Hot Pockets were in the freezer. *Good Will Hunting* was in theaters, while *Dharma & Greg* was on TV. Michael Jordan and the Bulls were still the kings of basketball. And you might have been getting sick and tired of paying late fees at your local Blockbuster.

A new start-up company felt your pain. This company hated late fees, too. Realizing that DVDs weigh a lot less than those old, clunky VHS tapes, this company wondered, *Why can't we just mail them and kill this whole late fee thing?* And that's exactly what they did. This company started mailing folks DVDs.

Their ability to see beyond the status quo did not stop there. The Internet had recently arrived, so they leveraged their own website—and changed how the world felt about in-home enter-tainment. Instead of renting out movies one at a time, in 1999, the company introduced an unlimited viewing, monthly sub-scription model. It didn't seem like that big of a change—but it was huge. This was the in-home entertainment super-sized value meal merged with the DoorDash moment.

For a century, people had been limited to selecting and paying for entertainment on an experience-by-experience basis. One movie ticket. One DVD. One option. Now a company offered unlimited entertainment, giving users no limits on how much they could watch each month. It was convenient. It was easy. It was affordable. And it meant there was no going back.

The world continued to change as information moved faster and

faster while customers grew hungrier for more unlimited entertainment. And they wanted it now: a new, super-duper-sized
value meal. The company capitalized on this, and introduced
streaming content around 2007. No more mailing DVDs, just
push a button and watch movies and shows streamed to your
home computers, TVs, and phones.

That might have been enough, but now this company realized
that the movie industry and studios hadn't evolved with the
changing times. They were inefficient, bloated, and controlling.
So this company did what smart companies do. They created
an opportunity from a glaring movie industry weakness. They
began curating their own world-class content by giving editorial
control and direction back to directors and actors, who fled the
studios for the increased creative freedom and lack of red tape—
not to mention, bigger bags of money. This company started
skipping the movie theaters altogether. And by toppling that
last domino, the company changed the world of entertainment
forever.

This company was, of course, Netflix. Thanks to Netflix, unlimited movies, shows, and other content are not only continually
available to viewers, but this kind of access has become the new
normal. It is expected. There is no going back to rewinding
VHS tapes, dealing with scratched-up DVDs, or renting movies
one at a time.

I know: *Why's Greg talking about movies again?* I share this fun story
because it's the tale of a couple of people who noticed the world
changing and had an idea. They saw that the market was broken
and that an industry wasn't willing to change.[61] Blockbuster,
the movie studios, and the whole entertainment industry were

too stubborn and too rich to try and evolve. And look what has happened. Big studios are scrambling to find lost profits. Movie theaters are closing all across the country. And Blockbuster is out of business.

An ironic side note: About ten years before Blockbuster shut their doors for good, Blockbuster was offered the chance to buy Netflix for just $50 million. They declined, supposedly laughing at the idea.

Well, who's laughing now? Netflix is one of the most powerful and influential companies in the world. It's worth around $100 billion.

The story of Blockbuster is no different than the RFA and financial industry story we told in Part I of this book. Both industries had grown bloated, resisted change, ignored their clients, and hoped nobody would notice the world of other opportunities and improvements circulating around them. Both focused on profit reports rather than people. When retirees needed the RFA and financial industry to change with the times, their needs were—and continue to be—ignored. The retiree was abandoned, while RFAs continued to focus on themselves and their own bottom lines.

Change is hard. Change is scary. Change takes time. Netflix wasn't a hit straight out of the gate. Changing the financial industry won't happen overnight either. But it will change.

As we'll see in Part II, good people are waking up and realizing that the world has changed and that retirees need help. Just as we all threw away our old VHS and DVD players, it's time to throw away the old way of planning for retirement. And it's time to throw away your financial advisor. There's a new type of professional out there who is ready to put retirees' needs ahead of their own. Finally.

These professionals will be the Netflix of the financial services world. They will replace your RFA.

They are called Retirement Planners.

CHAPTER 6

———

CRACKING THE DAM

Hoover Dam is 726 feet tall, 1,244 feet long, 660 feet thick (more than the length of two football fields), and contains enough concrete to build a four-foot-wide sidewalk around the equator. It took 5,000 workers five years to finish. It remains one of the most impressive structures in the world, keeping over 248 square miles of water from flooding Las Vegas.[62]

But there is a bigger dam, larger than any other in the world. It stretches from Wall Street all the way into each home in our country, and it took forty years to build and maintain. Unlike Hoover Dam, it doesn't hold water.

It was built by RFAs for the financial services industry, and to keep out one thing: information.

The way information is transferred, limited, filtered, manipulated, and controlled shapes the world. And we know that accessing and understanding information are the two master keys to unlocking the secrets of the universe.

Or, put another way, information allows humans to make better life decisions. Before Johannes Gutenberg invented the printing press in the 1400s, only 30% of the European population was literate.[63] Anyone who could read had the ultimate trump card in life—and in business. Think about it. If you were part of the illiterate 70%, everything you *knew* was funneled through someone or something else. News, religion, entertainment, and work were conducted mostly with secondhand information. It's hard to fathom how much power controlling all the information gave a select few back in the day. Instead of relaying the truth, they could paraphrase, misconstrue, overcharge, or rewrite the world to suit their interests. It was this unchecked power over information that led to some of the worst episodes in history.

Bear with me for a second, but the position of illiterate individuals in the Middle Ages was not that much different from the position of retirees in the 1980s and 1990s. The main difference is that, while only 70% of people in the Middle Ages were illiterate, almost 100% of retiring America in the late 20th century was *financially* illiterate. And that meant that retirees were turning over the fate of their life savings to an RFA and industry that they neither knew nor understood anything about.

What? How? Why? And WTF?

Exactly.

This retiree financial illiteracy happened for two driving reasons.

First, financial literacy wasn't yet a necessary skill. As we've seen, retirement was a new thing. Many folks worked until they died. If they did make it to the golden finish line of retirement, most didn't have any assets to worry about anyway. If they were really lucky, they were able to rely on a pension that didn't require any know-how or action other than cashing a monthly check.

Second, there was no access to financial information. Even if they were curious about their retirement accounts, retirees had no access, no idea of what to look for, and no clue who to ask. They were bombarded with new concepts and tools—IRAs, 401(k)s, annuities, mutual funds, indexes—that might as well have been in another language. So the relevant information was easily controlled and manipulated by the financial industry and the RFAs to really exploit the hardworking, everyday retiree. What the industry charged, how they charged, why they charged, and what they were charging for all remained a mystery to retir-ees. There were no checks and balances to the RFA juggernaut.

The creation of the retirement information dam allowed an industry to become a trillion-dollar empire. And this monop-oly led to almost all the bad things that could still happen to retirees today:

- People losing their homes and life savings to pay for multi-year nursing home stays.
- Retirees losing 40% of their IRA accounts to Uncle Sam's taxes.[64]
- Folks losing close to half their life savings to a market crash.[65]
- Countless people losing hundreds of thousands of dollars to RFA costs and investment fees.

Retirees had a limited ability to understand their investment choices, taxes, planning strategies, fees, and expenses—because all the relevant retirement information was being kept on the wrong side of the dam.

It wasn't much different than the Middle Ages—a few leading the many, resulting in disaster. Opinions vary, but The Crusades led to at least a million deaths over the span of two hundred years, with few having any real idea of what they were fighting and dying to save.

And now, roughly a thousand years later, retirees are marching toward a similar cliff regarding their life savings. This inevitable outcome is due to an overreliance on and unthinking allegiance to local RFAs, who continue to control the information you need to make good decisions. They perpetuated their sensationalized status by taking credit for market wins and blaming market losses on, ironically, the market (not their investment selections or timing). RFAs were the only financially literate humans around who could explain to retirees where their life savings went, what investments were being sold, and how to literally take their own money out of their own accounts—all because they controlled the dam, which only led to further siloing of information and more confusion about RFAs' services and fees.

CONTROLLING INFORMATION

How could retirees crack this dam? The answer is simple, but not easy. By getting ahold of more information. Let's take a quick step back to look at the history of some of the tools we've used to chip away at ignorance.

I've mentioned the printing press, which was one of the most meaningful tools in information dissemination history. It not only allowed books to carry knowledge around the world, but it also eventually made them affordable and available to the masses. It was one of the most significant inventions of all time; it shifted access to information—and power—from the few to the many on an unprecedented scale. Books like the Bible, which had once taken hundreds of days to handwrite, could now be printed in hours. Eventually, the printing press led to public forums, such as newspapers, that in the mid-to-late 1800s gave large parts of the population access to relevant and timely information for the first time ever.

The next information revolution came with radio, which became a staple in most homes in the 1920s and 1930s. News and information became even more accessible, including to those who were illiterate. Radio was followed by the cornerstone of US culture, the television. Televisions became a permanent fixture in most homes by the 1960s, providing more information to individuals from all socioeconomic groups.

Despite the amazing advances in information technology in most forms of news and entertainment, the financial services industry was still able to keep its consumers in the dark until relatively recently. Don't forget, in the 1980s there were still only three network channels (and maybe PBS). Retirement topics and financial information were not on the TV menu. Going into the 1990s, retirees remained in the financial dark ages. They navigated their retirement journey with the help of quarterly RFA account statements, confusing graphs and charts, and some financial propaganda. Ultimately, no one really understood anything apart from the number at the bottom of their statement next to "Total Account Value." And that only really relayed whether their accounts went up or down. Any planning information, together with the fees being drained from these accounts, was still locked away. And the financial industry and RFAs held the only keys.

WWW

The information war finally started to tilt toward the retirees in the mid-to-late 1990s. It was time for the largest informational revolution of all time. The dynamite that finally cracked the dam of financial ignorance was... the Internet.

It's difficult to adequately describe the extent of this paradigm shift. Information began to seep through the dam, giving power back to the consumer from many corporate industries. When people started to see what was happening behind certain curtains, they weren't pleased. Many industries, empires, and retail staples were wiped out overnight: travel agencies, landline telephones, bookstores, CD stores, retail stores, and video stores (sorry, Blockbuster), to name only several. In their place, a new genre of business emerged based on e-commerce that now comprises some of the world's largest and most successful companies.

Got it. No more rotary telephones and travel agents. But how did that change the financial services industry and RFAs? It started a period of transition for retirees that has been going on for around twenty years.

It took people some time to gain access to the right data, and then start to ask the right questions so as to understand what was going on under the hoods of their retirement accounts. It has been slow, getting retirees access to the right information, largely because the financial industry and RFAs have continued to spread propaganda and fear while constantly changing their language and systems to keep retirees confused and leverage their continued informational disadvantage.

But it was too late: the dam had cracked. Information about real and relevant retirement topics is now readily available. Retirees are exiting the Financial Dark Ages and moving into their very own Age of Enlightenment—or, better yet, their Age of Information. The Internet has given retirees access to new investment options, retirement strategies, tax plans, alternative fee plans, and legal tools.

The information is out there. Any retiree can now see what is going on in the retirement world around them. But it's still difficult to know what to do with all this new information. The world changed while they were asleep, and retirement changed with it. But people's retirement plans, together with their RFAs and the financial industry, haven't changed at all. RFAs are still using their 1980s playbook.

Change takes a little time. Getting the information. Understanding the information. Acting on the information. This stuff takes a minute—and don't think a trillion-dollar industry is going to just roll over and die without a fight for your retirement dollars.

Remember, it took almost *four hundred* years for the printing press to make waves when it came to literacy and getting information out to the masses.[66] In the next few chapters, I'm going to do my best to speed things up by telling retirees how they can achieve meaningful change for their retirement dollars.

CHAPTER 7

SNOOZE BUTTON

Snow White was out for one year. John Spartan (Demolition Man) was on ice for close to forty. And Steve Rogers (Captain America) was frozen for almost seventy. But Princess Aurora (Sleeping Beauty) wins the snooze button award for being asleep for a full century. My point—other than staying away from poisoned apples, a blond-haired Wesley Snipes, experimental drone plane trips over the North Atlantic, and dodgy spinning wheels—is that the world keeps going, with or without you. When you eventually wake up, the world you knew is gone—and you find yourself in a very different place and time.

That has never been truer for retirees. They can't afford to hit the snooze button again. The financial dam has broken. It's time to wake up in this scary new world.

BEEP. BEEP. BEEP.

Information is flooding everywhere across the Internet—and it's waking retirees up from a decade-long hibernation. Fee schedules, investment comparisons, tax plans, and long-term care realties are finally out in the open for everyone to see. Now, for the first time, retirees can start asking their RFA the right questions:

- What am I really paying for my RFA and his investments?
- What services am I getting?
- When should I pay taxes on my IRA?
- What about a nursing home event?
- Do I really need to be in the market at my age?

These are all great questions, and the right questions. This is what retirees need to know. And their newfound curiosity regarding RFA services and plans came about thanks to financial information being available to the masses for the first time in history.

Now that the snoozing was over, retirees began to raise some eyebrows and dig deeper into the stories being told by their local RFAs. This was tough. Many times, it was like finding out that a friend was disloyal, or not the person these retirees thought they knew. It hurt. And it led to confusion, denial, frustration, anxiety, even anger. Retirees were conditioned to believe that their RFAs walked on water, that they were superheroes, trusted advisors who were the saviors of their retirement. They were neighbors, deacons, perhaps even friends.

It's no surprise that questioning someone you have trusted with your life savings for numerous years is difficult.

I want to make it less uncomfortable for you.

Remember, your RFA isn't mowing your yard, or bagging your groceries. Your RFA is literally responsible for you and your family surviving the descent from retirement mountain with your life savings intact. I hope that empowers you to ask a few simple questions, but I know that is easier said than done. We all tend to make decisions based on emotion rather than reason—and RFAs are world-class relationship builders and defenders. Not to mention that they hold doctorates in manufacturing trust and loyalty among their clients and, let's not forget, bullshitting.

Ironically, however, they rarely have any advanced degrees in the skills and services that would help protect your money—you know, like financial and retirement planning.

THE END OF AN AGE

In better news, the age of the RFA is coming to an end. The snooze button that kept everyone in the dark ages, with no access to information, is gone. So you shouldn't feel bad about turning the tables and asking your RFA the right questions. If you need some direction, see Appendix A. It outlines some vital questions that every retiree should ask their RFA.

To help, I am going to share the largest changes to the retirement world that have happened between 1980 and the present. To make it easier (and to keep this chapter under a thousand pages), I'll break the changes into the four areas that are most critical to retirement planning:

1. Investments
2. Fees
3. Taxes
4. Long-Term Care

These are not just the areas that have experienced the most change and evolution during the forced retiree hibernation; they also remain the cornerstones of any successful retirement plan.

INVESTMENTS

If you don't keep your money under your mattress, it's invested. There are thousands of investments out there. I am going to trim them down into five broad categories:

1. Equities (stocks, ETFs, mutual funds)
2. Bonds (debt instruments)
3. Insurance (annuities and life insurance)
4. Commodities (metals and agricultural products)
5. Cash/cash equivalents (money market accounts, savings, and certificates of deposit)

(I know I've left some off the list, but they're not particularly relevant for this chapter, so all you crypto-junkies, relax.)

Before the age of the RFAs, investment choice didn't matter for most retirees. You retired. You received a monthly pension. The end. It didn't matter how your pension was invested or performed so long as your monthly check arrived on time. Once the IRA came around and pensions started to die, that all changed. Retirees had to choose their own investments or, more likely, pay someone to choose for them.

We saw earlier how RFAs owned every hot dog stand in every city. And the RFAs' focus was—and remained—selling a ton of very expensive hot dogs (a.k.a., actively managed mutual funds).

Around 1980, less than 6% of the US population owned an actively managed mutual fund, which meant that the number of mutual fund industry shareholders totaled around 11 million.[67] Yet now, 45.4% of US households, almost half of America, have been sold a mutual fund.[68] That is around eight times the growth while you were sleeping. Again, that is a ton of freaking over-priced hot dogs.

What changed once retirees woke up to what was going on? Thanks to the Internet splashing all this useful, real financial information on retirees' faces like cool water at an oasis, the performance of and fees associated with actively managed mutual funds were put under a microscope for the first time in over twenty years—and retirees didn't like what they saw. The fees were much higher and the performance much lower than they had been promised, particularly when compared with all the new and cheaper investment alternatives popping up every day.

The result? A new and more cost-effective way to participate in the stock market was born. To the chagrin of the RFAs selling mutual funds, this was a far better tool. An investment that cost less and earned more. A real win-win for retirees.

It's called "passive investing." In a nutshell, you invest in the market versus one stock. Now, this concept has been around awhile. Fifty years ago, it was the subject of Burton Malkiel's book *A Random Walk down Wall Street*. Malkiel observed—and quantified with evidence—that stock pickers can't consistently beat the market. Ever. Which more or less debunked the stockbroker's entire profession.[69]

Clearly, nobody listened.

Except for Jack Bogle. You know Jack, the freaking founder of Vanguard. The guy who first said, "Don't look for the needle in the haystack. Just buy the haystack."[70] Vanguard created the first index mutual fund in 1975.[71] These index funds usually own the major stocks aligned with certain indexes such as the S&P 500, Dow Jones, and so on. Then, around 1990, another pro-retiree investment option came along called "exchange-traded funds" (ETFs). Like index funds, this new investment option could mimic an index.[72]

I am not going to open Pandora's box by claiming that both these new options consistently outperform RFAs' stock-picking advice—especially after factoring in the cost of active management expenses and the RFA's 1% wrapper fees—although I could, and they do. But I am not going down that road because I believe retirees should focus on absolute certainties, and that performance charts and percentages can be manipulated and argued over endlessly. Instead, I want simply to show you how retirees have felt about index funds and ETFs after waking up over the last couple decades.

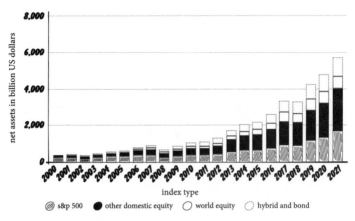

Total Assets in Index Funds

"Net Assets of Index Mutual Funds in the United States from 2000 to 2021, by Index Type," Statista, July 4, 2022, https://www.statista.com/statistics/1263833/net-assets-index-mutual-funds-type-usa/.

Index funds are retirement-appropriate, cost-effective, simple, and don't require active management. Where the index goes as a whole, you go too. That is why index funds have jumped from less than $400 billion in 2000 to almost $6 trillion twenty years later, as noted in the chart above. They were created to cut costs and help everyday folks participate in the market without helping a Wall Street mutual fund manager buy another Caribbean island.

Not kidding about the island joke, by the way. Did you know that *certain hedge fund managers make over a billion dollars EVERY YEAR?*[73] That is what happens with trillions of retirement dollars when nobody knows what is being charged or by whom.

Total Assets in ETFs

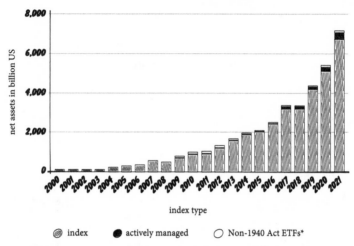

index type

index · actively managed · Non-1940 Act ETFs*

"Total Net Assets under Management (AUM) of Exchange Traded Funds (ETFs) in the United States from 2000 to 2021, by Type of Management," Statista, July 4, 2022, https://www.statista.com/ statistics/1263421/total-net-assets-etfs-management-type-usa/.

ETFs wanted in on this new retirement action, too. As you can see in the chart above, ETFs didn't exist before 1990—and by 2020, they comprised over $7 trillion of the US investment market. That is something like 10,000% growth in twenty-one years. It's clear that the retirees have spoken, because they are all starving for easier and cheaper ways to ride the market roller-coaster. And for once, the sheer force and volume of the information flooding the market forced the financial industry to cave in and finally deliver index-driven ETFs—much to the detriment of your local RFA's bank account.

If you do the math, the largest problem for RFAs is that index funds and ETFs can be purchased and managed with the ease of a click on any online platform. And given their nature, there is no management or additional trading needed. The customer just passively rides the index until they want to hop off, and it can all be done without any RFA fees or costs.

Active vs. Passive Investments in US

"Distribution of Active and Passive Investment Funds in the United States in 2011 and 2021, by Type," Statista, June 28, 2022, https://www.statista.com/statistics/1262209/active-passive-investment-funds-usa/.

This final chart, above, illustrates where the world is heading. Retiree dollars are going into passive investment options like index funds and ETFs, and running away from the overpriced hot dogs (actively managed accounts and mutual funds) sold by RFAs. Retirement dollars going into index funds have almost doubled from 2011 to 2021, and retirement dollars going into ETFs have more than doubled during that time, whereas expensive mutual funds are going the opposite direction, falling from 79% to 57% over the same time period. Clearly, there are many more retirement-friendly options now—while the hot dogs being sold by RFAs cost too much and perform too little.

Access to this information via the Internet finally gave retirees the opportunity to see the shortcomings of the investments they were being sold, which in turn led to huge opportunities for improvements, and for the pro-retiree financial industry to capitalize on a new way of thinking about investments.

I won't spoil the fun and get into all of the new and improved pro-retiree investment options here—I will in later chapters, I promise—but safe to say, the snooze button is permanently broken and once foggy-eyed retirees are looking around. They are finding a new smorgasbord of investment options that didn't exist twenty years ago. When you learn about them, you might just feel like you did as a kid, when you saw that glorious Ponderosa salad bar for the first time.

At the end of the day, all these new investment options evolved and changed, thanks to retirees' access to new information. This showed not only that there were other options out there, but also that retirees were being wildly overcharged for regular ol' hot dogs. Which leads us right into the next section.

FEES

The black hole for most retirees is fees. When you ask someone how much they pay their RFA, 99% of the time they have no idea how much comes out of their account every year. Even if they know the percentage going to the RFA, they have no clue how much that means in dollars, let alone actual investment costs. Does this approach or mentality apply to anything else in life? An oil change? Lawn care? Tax returns? Groceries? Of course not. One of my primary missions with this book, outside of convincing you to fire your financial advisor, is to bring to an abrupt end this phenomenon of needlessly giving away your retirement dollars.

Earlier, we dove into the origins and flaws of RFAs' investment fees and expenses. Here's a quick reminder. There are two fees: (1) what you pay your RFA to sell you an investment, and (2) the ongoing cost of the investments (mutual fund, variable annuity, etc.) they sell you.

The financial services world has kept a tight lid on *how* they take money out of your retirement accounts, and despite the Internet boom, not much has changed there. Retirees still run into detours and Do Not Enter signs when it comes to finding out who is taking money out of their accounts, when it happens, and how much.

Despite all the information out there that retirees can get for free, the average fee for RFA advice remains around 1.17%.[74] Sadly, when it comes to services, this still only buys you investment-picking—which itself continues to be commodified through technology and passive investment options. Meanwhile, the old RFA guard keeps digging in and, shockingly, going in the opposite direction by charging even higher fees.

OLD RFA MODEL	ANNUAL WRAP FEE	ANNUAL/LIFETIME[75] $500,000 ACCT. VALUE	ANNUAL/LIFETIME $1,000,000 ACCT. VALUE
Fisher Investments	1.25%	$6,250/$156,250	$12,500/$312,500
Edward Jones	1.41%–1.37%	$7,075/$176,875	$13,725/$343,125
Edelman Financial	1.65%–1.38%	$8,250/$206,250	$13,875/$346,875
Wealthfront & Betterment (Robo-Advisor Model)	.25%	$1,250/$31,250	$2,500/$62,500

All data provided in this table is from www.smartasset.com

If you are a retiree with a $500,000 IRA, I would look at this chart again. And if, after rereading it, you still struggle to get your head around the fact that you pay your Edward Jones RFA $13,725 a year, or $343,125 over the course of retirement: So. Do. I.

If we add up the time spent for a quick birthday call, one or two meetings, and pushing a button for an automated allocation program based on your age a couple times a year (a.k.a., the sell more mutual funds program), it would be *extremely* generous to say that your RFA is putting an annual ten hours into your family and plan.

Applying an hourly rate, that means you are paying your RFA around $1,372.50 per hour. Let that sink in. And let's not forget, they are *only* picking investments, not offering other professional services like legal or tax help or addressing any of the other big risks in retirement. They are still just selling mutual funds, forty years later. Thanks, Cousin Eddie.

The retirees waking up to this nightmare aren't where they wanted to be after half a century, but there are some glimmers of hope. A new type of investment-picker has arrived on the scene to dethrone the RFAs. And—spoiler alert—it's not a human.

It's not C-3PO, the Terminator, or Johnny 5. It's Mr. Robo-Advisor.

Robo-advisors have emerged over the last ten years as a much more cost-effective and transparent investment-platform option. They use algorithms and other technology to efficiently manage portfolios and leverage capital gains tax-harvesting techniques, amongst other nifty innovations. Currently, the biggest players in this robo-business are Vanguard Robo-Advisors, Schwab Intelligent Portfolios, Betterment, and WealthFront.[76]

If you want someone to put your money on the blackjack table (a.k.a., the stock market), do it more cost-effectively, and, in my humble opinion, with a higher likelihood of better returns, this is the route to take.

If RFAs are the world's most expensive VHS players from the Blockbuster days, robo-advisors are the first Blu-ray DVDs.

CAUTION: Robo-advisors still only pick investments. I am not advocating for them as a one-stop solution to get you safely down retirement mountain. Like RFAs, they don't help with all the other huge retirement risks that require real services and planning support. They are just a cheaper casino if you want to bet on the market with your retirement dollars.

As noted in the previous table, the annual cost of using a robo-advisor versus Edward Jones is $2,500 compared to $13,725. That is over $10,000 of savings a year, or almost $300,000 in savings over a thirty-year retirement. Those are some really expensive birthday calls, holiday dinners, and coffees with your RFA. Think about what you could do with an extra quarter of a million dollars in your account.

Although the RFAs are still hanging onto their model of charging 1% for their advice, the breaking of the information dam has done a great job of cutting into the world's most expensive hot dog-selling racket. Investment management for the masses has started getting cheaper.

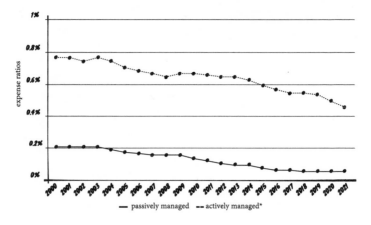

Mutual Fund Expense Ratio Costs

— passively managed -- actively managed*

"Expense Ratios of Bond Mutual Funds in the United States from 2000 to 2021, by Fund Management Type," Statista, July 4, 2022, https://www.statista.com/statistics/331807/expense-ratios-bond-mutual-funds-usa-by-fund-management-type/.

The actively managed mutual funds' expense ratios have taken a monstrous hit, thanks to retirees getting access to more information and more alternatives. Mutual fund expense ratios have been halved from 2000 to 2021, from almost .8% to around .4%. When you're talking about a retiree's $500,000 IRA, that is $2,000 staying in an account annually, or $50,000 over a retirement. Not only have the internal expense ratios been cut, the age of selling front-, middle-, and back-loaded mutual fund fees is also nearly dead and gone. A number of stubborn RFAs are still trying to hang on and sell A-share mutual funds (like American Funds), hoping that no one is looking so they can squeeze out a few more years of 5% commissions. But that heyday is over. RFAs are pivoting out of the mutual fund commission business and crowding their way into the 1% wrapper fee parking lot, which will be the last place they can try and continue to screw over retirees. This will be their last stand, the final battle the RFA will wage against you, the retiree.

Seriously, there are too many other options out there for you to keep wildly overpaying your RFA. And the world has changed in ways that require more services than these RFA hot dog sellers can provide, particularly when it comes to long-term care and taxes.

LONG-TERM CARE

You don't want to talk about it. You don't want to think about it. *Because it is never going to happen to you.* That is the mindset of almost every retiree I have ever met when I bring up the potential future need for a nursing home. Believe me, I get it. Getting old sucks. And nobody wants to plan for something they have convinced themselves they will never need.

Yet you have to talk about it. No one plans for their house to burn down, but you still carry homeowners' insurance, right? If you want a real plan for retirement, long-term care can't be ignored. It is too important. It costs too much. It could impoverish you or your spouse in just a few short years. Let me show you how by sharing some scary numbers.[77]

- 70%: the odds you will need some form of long-term care after the age of sixty-five
- 2.2 years: the average stay in a nursing home for a male
- 3.7 years: the average stay in a nursing home for a female

And the worst part is the cost. Take a look at this table.

Nursing Home Expenses in US

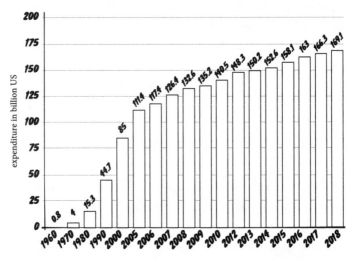

"Nursing Home Expenditure in the United States from 1960 to 2018 (in Billion U.S. Dollars)," Statista, March 15, 2021, https://www.statista.com/statistics/184780/us-nursing-home-expenditures-since-1960/.

It truly is unbelievable. The amount spent on long-term care, EVERY YEAR, has risen from $15 billion to $169 billion in forty years. Before most of you were lulled to sleep by the financial services industry, it cost about $10,000 a year if you went to a nursing home. Now that you've woken up and can see the information for yourself, it can be $9,000 a month ($108,000 a year), or more.[78] That means that if you and your spouse hit the averages above and you both end up having a prolonged nursing-home stay, you could be spending over $1,000,000 on the nursing home alone.

WTF?

How did this happen?

The good news first: We are all living longer. The bad news: You now need more help as you age. Cognitive disorders such as dementia and Alzheimer's are now much more common. And these diseases require more support and longer stays in nursing homes for those who are physically healthy but can't live alone.

The costs are staggering—and it's getting worse. Imagine what those costs could be in the next ten or twenty years. And Medicare doesn't pay for care longer than one hundred days in Ohio, for example, so needing long-term care could mean you lose everything you worked your whole life to build, leaving little to your surviving spouse and nothing to your kids and grandkids. That doesn't feel like the grand, "holistic" plan promised to most retirees by their RFAs. Yet, shockingly, this risk is swept under the rug by almost every RFA.

Next question. Why the heck didn't your RFA talk to you about the largest risk to your retirement?

I can't say for sure, but let me take a crack at why I think your RFA swept some of this under their rug.

- RFAs don't want to talk about nursing homes because it is tough and could upset you. It is much easier to focus on fun investment, travel, and grandkid talk.
- RFAs don't have any expertise in, or knowledge or understanding of, how Medicaid spend-down and long-term care planning works, or how asset protection trusts can help.
- RFAs know that almost nobody wants to buy long-term care insurance because it's too expensive or too hard to qualify—fewer than 5% of Americans have it (and that number continues to decline).[79]

- RFAs know it won't be their problem, and play the odds. If an RFA brings on a retiree and sells them investments, there is usually a good chance that RFA will be retired themselves before their client has a long-term care issue. That is a super shitty thing even to think might be true, let alone risk a client's life savings on. But admit it, it makes a little sense, doesn't it?

When that unexpected prognosis, broken hip, or other family tragedy occurs, there is no rug big enough to hide it under, and no plan to avoid losing everything.

A *real* retirement guide, who accepts responsibility for securing and protecting your life savings and the financial prosperity of your family, isn't always going to be able to talk about the fun stuff. They must introduce the hard and uncomfortable conversations, too. This is a real issue, and there are some very effective new strategies and tools to protect your assets, spouse, and family from this huge long-term care risk. And these new strategies aren't about investments. As we'll see in Chapter 10, they involve asset-protection trusts and attorneys.

But the reason most people haven't heard about these options and strategies is, they take a lot more work to learn about and put into motion. And they don't end with yet another investment sale or commission for your RFA, so under the rug these possible solutions go again.

TAXES

Death and taxes. Both bummers, but inevitable. Republican or Democrat, it doesn't usually matter; *almost* nobody likes the idea of giving more money to Uncle Sam. The creation and evolution of the IRA has left a Grand Canyon-like fault line in most retirees' plans—and it could be the difference between paying $50,000 or $200,000 out of your IRA accounts to taxes!

Before I show you this tax time bomb that is set to detonate in your very own IRA account, let's outline some tax basics:

- 401(k) accounts are sponsored by your employer; they take money out of your paycheck before it gets taxed.
- IRA accounts can be created on your own, or when you roll your 401(k) account out of your employer plan and into your personal management, but they are more or less the same as a 401(k) from a tax perspective.
- All "pre-tax" retirement accounts owe tax [401(k), IRA, etc.]. There is no way around it: Uncle Sam will always collect from you, your spouse, or your kids. The only question is how much and when.
- Any money that comes out of a pre-tax account is treated as income, added to your 1040 tax return, and taxed at your retiree income tax rates.
- Roth accounts mean you already paid tax and the money is growing tax-free. There is no tax consequence for pulling money out, other than the fact that it will no longer grow tax-free.
- Retirees don't have to take money out of their pre-tax accounts until they reach age seventy-two.
- At seventy-two, retirees have to take out required minimum draws each year based on their life expectancy.
- A widow or widower can inherit a pre-tax account, roll it over to themselves, and wait until they are seventy-two to draw from it, too, even if their deceased spouse was over seventy-two at the time of the rollover.

- Kids who inherit their parents' IRAs must immediately start taking draws from the IRA every year and deplete it to zero within ten years.
- Kids pay income tax at each kid's own income tax rate, not Mom and Dad's rate.

Clearly, in the 1980s, this wasn't on retirees', or any RFA's, radar. Why? Well, nobody'd had time to accumulate any wealth yet, because they were just starting to fill up these IRA accounts. They were empty or small and the owners were thirty years from retirement, so the tax significance was little to none. Safe to say, when your alarm clock recently started beeping, all of that changed.

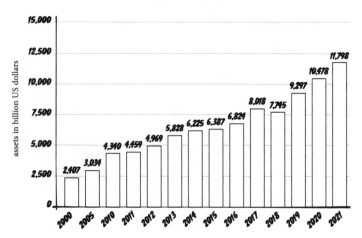

Traditional IRA Growth in US

"Total Assets of Traditional Individual Retirement Accounts in the United States from 2000 to 2021," Statista, July 20, 2022, https://www.statista.com/statistics/187894/traditional-ira-total-assets-in-the-us-since-2000/.

This chart above shows a whole bunch of IRA account growth. I know, what is the big deal? Everyone has a larger IRA account now than they did back in the 1980s. So what? Everyone should be happy. Don't we all just have more money?

That's true, but it's also quite a bit more money waiting in the queue to get taxed. And while we're talking about all those soon-to-be-taxed dollars, doesn't anyone else find it curious that if someone has a $500,000 IRA, Uncle Sam doesn't want to start getting paid back on that lifetime tax loan until they reach seventy-two? For one thing, it seems like a long time to wait. For another, when you start paying back Uncle Sammy, he only wants about 3.6% back from the principal at age seventy-two ($500,000/27.4 life expectancy). Hopefully, your money is growing faster than 3.6% a year—and when you reach the age of eighty, Sam is still only asking for about 4.9% of your pre-tax account back each year. Weird, right? (I stopped looking after eighty because the average life expectancy in America is less than eighty.)[80]

Anyhow, what does this mean? Is Sam just a nice guy? Is this our federal government operating on altruism and not caring how much or when it gets repaid? The way the system is set up means there is literally no mathematical way the government will get paid back during a retiree's lifetime. Actually, quite the opposite. This system is built so that the pre-tax IRA accounts are actually growing bigger, not smaller, in retirement. Are you still confused?

I'm not surprised. This diabolical rope-a-dope plan was Uncle Sam's vision all along.

Let me try to explain. Let's say you own an apple tree and I own a warehouse. My fee for storing your apples is five apples a year for every hundred apples stored. This is a great deal, right? No fees or interest? But you (hopefully) ask, "What's the catch? When does my fee start?" I reply that I am such a nice guy, I won't start taking five out of every hundred apples every year until you are seventy-two. Wow, what a great deal. But did you read the fine print? You didn't realize that the deal you cut might be pretty good while you and your spouse are still alive, but that when one spouse dies, the warehouse will start charging double: now the fee is ten apples for every hundred stored. Nor did you grasp that when both of you die, your kids will pay quadruple *that* fee, ending up having to pay the warehouse forty apples for every hundred apples stored. That's almost half your lifetime stash of apples going to me.

Does kicking your tax payments down the road still feel like a good idea? No! It's a terrible deal. Well, it's exactly what's happening if you have no plan for your IRA or are just waiting to take the required annual minimum in retirement when you get to age seventy-two.

Now, here is how Uncle Sam gets away with it.

A reminder: You are *always* going to pay income tax on your pre-tax IRA accounts. The only questions are (1) when, and (2) how much. When you retire, your income goes down, which in turn means that your tax rates go down. Let's take a quick look at the current federal income tax brackets:

2022 US Federal Tax Brackets

Tax Rate	Taxable Income (single)	Taxable Income (married filing jointly)
10%	up to $10,275	up to $20,550
12%	$10,276 to $41,775	$20,551 to $83,550
22%	$41,776 to $89,075	$83,551 to $178,150
24%	$89,076 to $170,050	$178,151 to $340,100
32%	$170,051 to $215,950	$340,101 to $431,900
35%	$215,951 to $539,900	$431,901 to $647,850
37%	over $539,900	over $647,850

Kemberley Washington, "2022–2023 Tax Brackets and Federal Income Tax Rates," *Forbes*, last modified November 7, 2022, https://www.forbes.com/advisor/taxes/taxes-federal-income-tax-bracket/.

In the United States, we have a graduated tax system. That means everyone's dollars are taxed the same going up the tax rate ladder. Take this example: You make $50,000 a year, your neighbor makes $500,000 a year, and you are both single. Both of you will pay roughly 10% on the first $10,275. No difference, even though your neighbor makes ten times what you do. The next dollars over that amount would pay at the next tax bracket, and you keep going up until you reach your total income. Why is this important? Well, you are retired. Your income is most likely turned off, and you may not have turned on Social Security.

Regardless, you can now get your pre-tax dollars out of your IRA accounts at a huge discount—if you plan ahead and build a tax plan rather than use Uncle Sam's plan for your IRA dollars.

If you fall back asleep at the wheel or your RFA ignores the issue in the driver's seat, a couple things could happen. First, the "widow's penalty." When a spouse passes, whoever is left goes from married to single tax filing rates. As the table above shows, this can cause your tax rates to almost double in many circumstances. That surviving spouse is now getting double-dipped for dollars they may need for support in retirement.

Next, the "kiddo's penalty." When that surviving spouse passes, the money goes to the kids. And you know what, your kids are statistically in their highest earning years, which means they are in the highest tax brackets. Again, they have to start taking money out of all of your inherited IRA accounts immediately, and this IRA money is then added to your kid's income/salary too which will push them into even higher tax brackets—which means, after factoring in state taxes, that close to half your IRA could be rerouted back to Uncle Sam versus going to your spouse and kids.

Make sense now? Sam is a very patient but greedy uncle. And this is real dollars, too. For a $500,000 IRA account that you allow to fall into the *Widows Penalty*, you could end up paying around a 20% effective tax rate, or $100,000 over the course of the widow's or widower's life. Or, if it goes into the *Kiddos Penalty*, your kids could end up paying a 40% effective tax rate. That's $200,000 of the $500,000 IRA, going to the tax man.

Ironically, you can control this to the penny.

That's right. To win and beat the system, all you have to do is one simple thing.

PAY THE TAX.

It is unavoidable, but you can stick it to Uncle Sam by paying the taxes incrementally over five to ten years at your retired lower tax rates, on your terms. With a proper tax plan, we see IRA tax liability crashing down to 10 to 15% rates. Instead of losing $200,000 of your $500,000 IRA to taxes, you could walk away only paying $50,000. That is $150,000 of real tax savings.

Yet almost no RFAs put together these tax plans, despite the clear savings for their clients. Why? I am so glad you asked. I have a couple ideas about why your RFA ignores this huge retirement risk.

- RFAs don't get paid for tax planning. Tax planning takes time to assemble and build, and there is no investment to sell or commission to be made.
- RFAs don't have the expertise or knowledge to build a tax plan because they don't understand how taxes and Medicare work. (If they did, wouldn't this conversation already have happened?)
- RFAs don't want you to do it—because if you take money out of your IRA and pay tax on it, your accounts are smaller. Or, God forbid, you may actually spend and enjoy some of your after-tax money during your golden years. Either way, the RFA's 1% fee will be applied to that smaller amount after taxes or after you spend it, so your RFA takes a pay cut when you do IRA tax planning.
- RFAs ignore this on purpose. This is terrible, but hear me

out. They know the real burn of not planning for your IRA happens when both of you die, which could be twenty-plus years away—so why not just ignore it? The RFA knows that they will probably already be retired by the time that eventually happens.

I know the last point feels pretty sinister, but it goes back to the RFA approach to planning for long-term care costs, too. There is a good chance that your RFA will be retired before their tax planning miss will ever be an issue. RFAs keep encouraging their clients to wait until seventy-two and take the minimum in order to maximize their 1% fees.

The infamous question RFAs ask to try to keep all your money in that 1% account where it is: "Why would you want to pay taxes if you didn't have to? You know you can wait until you're seventy-two."

That remains the favorite staple argument among RFAs who want to get their clients to back off from the idea of tax planning. Sadly, some accountants take a similar approach. It feels lazy and self-serving. And it's complete rubbish. It defies both logic and simple math. It is just playing off of our emotions, our abhorrence of paying taxes. You *do* have to pay taxes, so why not control when you pay them and reduce the amount while you're at it?

I hope this chapter has shown you exactly why many RFA sermons are lazy and, frankly, horrendous investment, long-term care, and tax advice. Instead of someone who builds a plan geared toward keeping your dollars rolling to your RFA and Uncle Sam, you need someone who will help you build a specific plan for each of these risks.

The world has changed during nap time. Hopefully, all of these changes, and RFAs' unwillingness to embrace these opportunities, are yet more reasons for you to take a step closer to firing your financial advisor.

CHAPTER 8

THE LAST DANCE

There's a company that invented the first personal computer, laser printers, computer graphical interfaces, WYSIWYG text editor (a precursor to Microsoft Word), and the freaking Ethernet. No joke. Seriously, they more or less invented the Internet and personal computers. Remarkably, the same company filed for bankruptcy in 2000, exactly as the world transitioned to—wait for it—the Internet and personal computers. Meet Xerox, the company that could not see past the big photocopier dollars. They went the same route as Blockbuster and DVDs because they couldn't envision a future that was different from the past.

This is no different than RFAs' inability to see beyond mutual funds and stock-picking.

The "toner head" executives at Xerox blew it when it came to adapting to the changing world around them. There is a story in which Steve Jobs toured their facility in 1979 in exchange for Xerox getting to invest $1 million in Apple. The story goes that Jobs then had Apple incorporate everything he saw at the Xerox headquarters into Apple's own processes. That may or may not be true. But what is true is that Xerox was rendered so complacent by the huge copier dollars that had fueled them for decades that they missed the largest product and industry opportunity of the last century.

What happens when a business, or an entire industry, keeps its head in the sand for too long and ignores the needs of its consumers in a changing world? Well, for Blockbuster or travel agencies, it's the end of the road. They simply disappear for good. Companies such as United Airlines or Xerox file bankruptcy, do some restructuring, and get a do-over business mulligan. But in rare circumstances, when there is nowhere else for the consumer to turn and the industry is making so much money that it can't really change its path or walk away, the industry doubles down. It uses counteroffensive tactics. And that is exactly what RFAs have been doing since the dawn of the Internet.

Historically, one of the most effective offensive tactics is distraction. Misdirection. Bright lights. Noise. After all, humans are easily distracted, aren't we?

That's what the financial industry has done since 2000. RFAs have turned on the disco lights and cranked up the music. Their goal is simple: Do anything and everything to disorient their clients and distract them from what is happening. Use new verbiage, new products, and spurious certifications; rebrand old ideas, tangle up the fee structures, and do anything else that will encourage you to look away from your quarterly statement and stare instead at that shiny, spinning disco ball.

The financial services industry and RFAs are playing deejay. They know that the sand in their proverbial hourglass is running low. Commission-based mutual funds and variable annuities are on life-support. RFA fees and costs are receiving more and more scrutiny. Their cupboard is bare. They have no services to help retirees tackle what we've just shown you are the biggest risks: things like IRA tax planning and skyrocketing long-term care costs. Nor do they have any clue about the emergence of index funds, ETFs, and robo-advisors, all of which give the retiree more choices and charge fewer fees. The RFAs remain all-in on simply picking investments and charging that hefty 1% for the privilege.

It doesn't make sense. How are RFAs pulling this off? Well, a wild animal is at its most dangerous when it is wounded and cornered, and that's precisely where RFAs are today. The financial services industry is out of rope and on the spot, finally being forced to answer for the fees they charge in return for the services they don't provide.

How did the RFAs react to this existential threat? Get ready to boogie. They went on the offensive, turned up the music, and launched the world's largest and most expensive disco party of all time.

I have broken down the RFAs' *Top Five Greatest Hits* for you:

- Track 1: The [Insert Superlative Here] Financial Plan
- Track 2: Token Financial Deliverable
- Track 3: Fee-Only Saint
- Track 4: CFP Expert
- Track 5: Fiduciary Savior

TRACK 1: THE [INSERT SUPERLATIVE HERE] FINANCIAL PLAN

When you have to use a superlative to describe your product or services, it's a problem. Think about it. A service is described by what it should be or does, not as simply "awesome." The same goes for products. You don't see Porsche selling the "beautiful" Cayenne, or a law firm selling "enforceable" contracts, or an accountant advertising an "accurate" tax return. The product or service should stand on its own. The quality is inferred by the product or service.

That's the RFA's problem. If you are only selling investments, you don't have many other ways to describe your plan. The "sell and buy overpriced investments retirement plan" tagline doesn't have a great ring to it. So RFAs have to turn the music up. And the song that starts to play usually has lots of lyrics about "holistic" and "comprehensive" planning. You hear those terms over and over. Call me old-fashioned, but I always thought adjectives like those would be assumed by a retiree when they reviewed the list of services that was actually delivered—you know, if the plan was actually holistic and comprehensive.

This song should come with a "buyer beware" advisory. Whenever you hear or see the terms "holistic" or "comprehensive planning" being used by an RFA to describe what they do for you in retirement, I recommend simply asking them one of these questions: "What services and documents do your comprehensive services include?" or "Can I see a list of the holistic services that you do start-to-finish for me and my family?" You have to pin them down and dig in—they will always give you a nod and then deny that nod after you sign on the dotted line. For example, when they say they do tax planning, you need to drill down: "So you do my tax returns?" and "You build me an IRA tax plan that states when and how much to withdraw every year—and then manage it for me over my entire retirement?"

Prepare to watch your RFA squirm.

It is that simple, though. To call anything part of your services, you have to actually do it. You can't just talk about it or hand over a business card referral to a CPA or attorney down the street. "Holistic and comprehensive financial plans" is really code for: "We don't have any real or meaningful additional services to put on our website, so instead we are going to use platitudes and jargon." This bear trap includes passively referencing estate planning, Social Security, taxes, and other relevant topics, but all those references lead to a business card referral, not a solution to your problem. Another common RFA tactic is demonstrating a cursory knowledge of fancy legal, tax, and financial buzzwords without having any intention of turning any of those discussions into action plans over the course of your retirement.

The best you can hope for is a binder of documents you will never reference again after the RFA signs you up for their annual 1% fee—which is actually the next song on the playlist.

TRACK 2: TOKEN FINANCIAL DELIVERABLE

Sad statistical truth: If you are reading this book, you are probably paying your RFA more than $10,000 every year, or around $300,000 over your retirement. For that much money, you probably walked out of their office at the end of the sale process with something to show for it, right? At least something under your arm?

Cue volume increase and get ready for an avalanche of forecasts, charts, jargon, variations, budgets, and checklists, all mashed into your master financial-bullshit-book for the next thirty years. Oh boy.

The bait-and-switch goes a few ways. Either you buy the "financial plan," or you use their services and get a "financial plan," or they will do a "financial plan" at no cost and then you decide if you want to implement it. Whatever the exact approach, it's tailored to that ultimate RFA goal of getting a 1% fee out of your retirement account forever. Curiously, these fees are rarely outlined in these "comprehensive" financial plans. Weird.

It's kind of like when you purchase a new vehicle from different model options: cars, trucks, or SUVs. Financial plans have a couple models that RFAs like to sell. The "kitchen sink' model is a very popular approach. It's an overstuffed hundred pages of fill-in-the-blank boilerplate forms, 78% of which have nothing at all to do with you or your goals, but it sure looks big and full stuffed with all that paper. Then we have the "simplified check-list" model. Retirees love checklists, so this is the never-ending running tally of to-dos. Again, it's just a form that has little tailoring to your situation or information involving anything to do with your biggest concerns in retirement. But man, it is fun to check those darn boxes.

The "income plan" model of financial plan deliverables takes the cake. Running out of money is retirees' biggest fear and the RFA knows it—and leans into it. "We need to make sure you have income for the rest of your life." No shit. I always laugh when I see a thirty-year income plan, though. Do you see and appreciate how completely insincere and disingenuous this RFA deliverable really is? Think on it with me. Most folks literally have no idea where they are eating lunch the next day, let alone outlining this brand-new retirement thing for the rest of their freaking lives. Trying to fill in thirty years of projected travel, income, spend-ing, returns, and expenses (known and unknown)? Goodness. It is not a very useful exercise. Nor is it an accurate one. But it does make you *feel* better, seeing it in writing.

And the worst feature of this income model financial plan is the "guaranteed for life" income ~~promise~~ scam. Most times, this comes in the form of an income rider sold on a new annuity as part of this master plan. Now, I do *love* simple, predictable, low-cost and safe annuities—but I hate annuity riders. Why?

You are paying an annual fee, often around 1%, to the insurance company. And why? *To pay yourself back your own money over twenty years.*

It's true. Most riders pay you 5% of your principal balance back year after year. Do the math. Or in fact, let me do the math for you.

Using an annuity rider, it would take at least twenty years to get your money back (5% × 20 years = 100%). So if you give an RFA $100,000, the income rider will charge 1% for twenty years ($20,000), and you will get $5,000 paid back to you each year for the following twenty years. If you outlive the life expectancy tables, you might win. I know they promise it will pay forever, but almost nobody turns it on until it's too late in life to get any real value from it. RFAs and insurance companies know this fact and are counting on you dying long before the insurance company stops paying you back your own money and has to start using the insurance company's own dollars. It's a great deal—for the insurance company. And if you don't make it twenty years, they can even keep the balance!

Around 99% of income riders never get turned on.

All right, I made that up—but that has to be close to accurate. Do you have an income rider? And is it turned on? I'm guessing the answer is nope. Yet you are still paying that 1% fee for the privilege, every year. Why? Running out of money is your biggest fear—and it is also the biggest lie told by the industry. Seriously, how many homeless folks do you see on the side of the road with signs like My Income Plan Was Off By 4% or Inflation Screwed Me: That Extra 75 Cents a Gallon for Milk Did Me In!! You know the answer. People self-regulate their lives and spending.

Let's not pretend that you need to be babysat by RFAs to responsibly live your lives.

When people ask me about income plans, I give them the same advice. I tell them to add up all their accounts and then add in their annual income from Social Security, pensions, and anything else multiplied by thirty. That is your retirement war chest. Now divide the total by thirty years. Boom! That is an income plan that will give you a rough idea of how much you can spend each year based on average US life expectancy. And it also assumes your money doesn't grow one penny in retirement.

REMEMBER: You can only take income for assets that are in your account. Sounds simple, but this fact is ignored by RFAs every day. The risks we've already noted—like taxes and long-term care—can take from your savings and leave you with little or nothing, and we know that 5% of zero is zero. At that point, no income plan is going to be able to cut that check for you if all your assets are with the nursing home and Uncle Sam.

"So Greg, are you telling everyone to just ignore income and expense planning?" Of course not. I am just saying that income planning is not that complicated, and there is not much *anyone* (including an RFA) can do to change the reality of the size of your retirement accounts outside of telling you to work longer. That is the truth no RFA wants you to know. They can guarantee what comes out of your accounts (their fees), but nobody can forecast the future and timing of the roller-coaster market. It's really financial theater to play on your fear of running out of money. You have X and you spend Y every year. You live within your means. And guess what, that's what almost every retiree does.

The RFA deliverable is meant to overwhelm you, impress you, confuse you, and, most of all, sell you. It's certainly not intended to protect you. Creating a huge knot to untie is the real secret to this industry's scary sales method. Ironically, the RFA creates the knot.

It's terrible, but it's true. Like a spider's venom, the only real goal of your fancy financial deliverable is to paralyze you and keep you from going anywhere. Retirement planning does not live in a fancy binder. It is—or *should* be—real services and a real guide, who is with you every year, tackling the realities of your accounts and the world around you and helping you read all the new signs on your way down retirement mountain. It is iterative and ever-changing. That is retirement planning.

TRACK 3: FEE-ONLY SAINT

The underlying audacity of this chart-topping RFA hit—fee-only planning—is baffling and infuriating. The only thing worse than the gall of touting this as a "win" for retirees is its popularity among the retiree masses who have accepted and freaking celebrate it.

The most recent RFA battle cry is, "Commissions are evil!" Fee-only planning simply amounts to the RFA charging whatever fee they want—usually 1% of your account—regardless of work done. Every year. Forever.

Let's really think about this for a second.

The fee-only song and dance was really the RFAs' only available move and pivot. It's an all-in, Texas hold 'em play. They basically gave up even trying to hide the fact that all they do is sell investments without any other services or advice. They set out to try and convince you that charging an arbitrary 1% fee based on how many zeroes are in your account is a good thing, while paying a commission for anything is a sin.

That is the RFAs' entire argument. It has nothing to do with their services or how they can help you protect your retirement. They are bragging about how they charge you, not what they are doing for you. That's it.

This is something RFAs champion every day to their clients: "Hey Joe, if you have $100,000, you owe me $1,000 each year to pick some investments. But if you give me $200,000, you owe me $2,000. I do the exact same amount of work, but get paid twice as much with no other services. Don't worry, though. There are no commissions involved, so your retirement is in good hands."

The financial industry's best effort to put their trillions of profits to work is to slander their biggest competitor, and the biggest threat to them, for your retirement dollars: insurance companies (annuities). It's not a coincidence that the target is commission-based compensation for selling these annuities. But let's think about this together. The irony is that an insurance company charges in the same way as every other company on the planet. The RFA industry is the only professional service in the world that charges an arbitrary percentage regardless of how little they do—forever.

When you pay for a car, a house, a tax return, a power of attorney, a certificate of deposit (CD), or an iPhone, there is a "commission." In other words, there is a margin that is profit for the person providing the product or service. And the biggest rub of all is, when you buy most annuities, or a CD at the bank, the commission is paid by the insurance company or bank to the seller. It doesn't come out of your retirement dollars. This means you know exactly what terms and interest rates you get. The costs of that annuity and any payments to the person selling it are already factored into your advertised returns, with no additional fees. Your account balance doesn't go backwards forever from the day you buy it. Commissions are simple and transparent, with a finite cost to the consumer—which is why almost every other sales profession in the world uses them.

Commissions are the opposite of the perpetual drain of a 1% fee-only RFA arrangement that never stops taking money out of your account.

The fee-only song is a desperate, made-up marketing campaign used to try and change the narrative of an industry that refuses to change its services to accommodate retirees' real needs. And when this song stops and everyone's rushing to sit down, you'll be looking for more than the missing chair. You'll be looking for the missing part of your life savings.

Speaking of marketing campaigns, it's time for the two most frequently asked and yet least relevant questions in retirement planning. These tunes are played by the RFA over and over and over.

TRACK 4: CFP EXPERT

"Are you a CFP?"

Phew. Thank goodness. Those letters are like titanium around your savings. If you're a certified financial planner (CFP), you're in the coolest band of RFAs since the Beatles. It is so awesome to be able to tell people you work with a CFP. Your RFA is "certified." That's got to make you feel better already, right?

Are you sensing some sarcasm? Good. I am laying it on pretty thick.

I am, of course, a little wary. Before you put all your eggs (a.k.a., your life savings) into this basket due to three consonants on an overpriced business card, let me share the answers to the two most important questions you should ask about why RFAs want you to care so much about whether or not they are CFPs. First, who certifies them? And second, how do they get/keep certified? Let's keep that champagne on ice for a second.

Who determines who is certified? This arbiter of magical credentials must be credible, experienced, and impressive, right? Shoot, given that what is at risk is not a two-year warranty on your garage door-opener, but instead the wealth and life savings of the entire country, one would hope so. First guess, is it a federal government regulatory agency like FINRA or the SEC, someone overseeing the protection of consumers related to all things relating to securities? Nope.

Okay, well then it must be a state-by-state institution with experience protecting consumer rights, like possibly the Department of Insurance? Nope.

What else? Oh yeah, the education component. I guess this certification must have an educational affiliation with a famous school of business or finance? That would make sense. Nope again.

This "certification" comes from a private company—a "charitable" 501(c)(3) company, to be precise. Shockingly, this company has no regulatory or educational roots or affiliations. Your life savings are rubber-stamped by a freaking marketing company. That is the cold, hard truth. This company literally sells those three-letter marketing licenses to 80,000 RFAs at a recurring fee of $400 a year for the privilege. Yup, $30 million a year going to a rotating board of directors who, I would guess, are living their best lives while earning seven-digit salaries. They are in the marketing business of selling an acronym, not vetting RFAs to protect your life savings.[81]

So how do RFAs get those three marketing letters on their business cards? The barriers to entry are shockingly low: candidates with little to no actual client-facing experience could graduate college, join an RFA shop for two years (even as an apprentice), take the CFP course, pass the test, and become CFPs. The need for a bachelor's degree can even be waived for five years.[82]

Think about it. Why would a marketing sales company want to make it too hard to buy those three letters?

Congrats. Your retirement is now in the hands of a twenty-four-year-old who has never lived life, built and executed a retirement plan, or even run a client meeting by himself. But he has paid $400 to have "CFP" next to his name, the crown jewel of the financial vetting and validation process.

That should be scary for all retirees, but it isn't even the worst part of this CFP scam. The worst part is that the policing process is more or less self-reporting. What does that mean? It means that all CFPs really need to do is pay their annual fee. No matter how badly they screw up planning for retirees, no matter if they ruin the life savings and the lives of their clients, they'll keep their three letters. The entire system is contingent on tattletales reporting on other CFPs. And even then, nothing seems to happen.

It's a joke. This CFP factory has a history of bad press and scandals.[83] It is rarely talked about in financial circles (because they are all CFPs), but just hop on the Internet and type in "CFP scandal" or "CFP lawsuits" to see countless cases in which consumers sued an organization because they relied on those three letters and bad things happened to their retirement dollars. The company claims to audit and uphold the standards it proclaims, but it doesn't appear that way in practice. Very public records clearly show frequent, excessive violations and negligence by RFAs across the country who hold the CFP designation, with no disciplinary action taken to remove their CFP status.

Why? Because the core business was never about retirees—it was about selling more letters. For the last ten years, the CFP marketing company has spent around a third of its revenue—around $10 million *every* year—on nothing but marketing.[84] One hundred million in marketing dollars out the door in a decade: wow, what kind of a charity is that? They have no system, budget, or intention of ever upholding, enforcing, or policing the letters they sell. Their focus is on simply selling more letters.

Even if their auditing process was pristine—and it clearly is not—those three letters still wouldn't amount to anything more than a limited experience barrier and cursory knowledge of fancy estate planning and academic tax terminology earned through some online classes. They don't include any certifications regarding having real client experience delivering plans that work. Even including client reviews and testimonials on a CFP's website would be a huge asset of real-life value. But that doesn't happen—it's just those three letters on business cards, email signatures, pamphlets, and websites.

This popular song is a dangerous lullaby. Those three letters may be fun to talk about over a coffee with a neighbor. But buzzwords and a couple of online courses can't replace real experience and services that could actually protect your retirement. It's just a $30 million marketing machine that helps RFAs sell more 1% fees to retirees.

Well, if the CFP is the empty marketing certification, the last song we will talk about reads more like a Sunday sermon.

TRACK 5: FIDUCIARY SAVIOR

"Are you a fiduciary?"

The worldwide counteroffensive of the financial industry wouldn't be complete without a heavy dose of self-righteousness. The fiduciary figure has been anointed with such an exalted status that the public has been brainwashed into thinking that being a fiduciary is a vital requirement for the future holder of all their money. Real walking on water stuff. The Internet demands that any real financial sherpa be a fiduciary. The problem: 99.99% of retirees have no idea what being a fiduciary actually means. It's hilarious, right? Except the joke is on you.

Americans really love jargon—we eat it up. 5k televisions. 5G cell phones. Organic anything. Be honest, we really have no idea what any of this shit means, nor what its significance might be. But we will pay more for it, won't we?

I can't help you gauge the importance of TV resolution, cell service, or organic popsicles, but I can break down what it really means to be a fiduciary.

Let's start by getting those RFAs who are *not* fiduciaries out of the way:[85] any RFA who has a Series 6 or Series 7 license, a CFP designation, or an insurance license. You can have one of those fun collections of numbers and letters—hell, you can have all of them—but it doesn't matter. You are not a "fiduciary" according to the only governing bodies that matter, FINRA and the SEC.

You must hold a Series 65 or 66 license to be a "fiduciary."

Well, shoot. You have no idea what that *Series* thing means? That makes two of us, along with every other retiree.

After all the pious grandstanding, the brain trusts in Washington D.C. built two standards when it comes to making investment recommendations: a best interest standard and a suitability standard.

That's it. Two questions. Is a recommendation in the best interest of a client? That's the best interest standard. Is a recommendation suitable for a client? That's the suitability standard. Of course, the best interest standard is the fiduciary standard (eye roll).

The best interest standard is an insincere promise championed by RFAs and the financial services lobby to make it seem as if their advice is superior to the advice given out by their closest and largest competitor, the insurance industry. The RFA world needed to drive a wedge to protect their 1% monopoly, and they succeeded. They made it the *law* that if someone gets a commission, they cannot be a fiduciary. How convenient. The fiduciary gods (i.e., the RFA industry) has ensured that anyone who sells an annuity—no matter how much sense it makes or how cost-effective it is for a client—can never wear the fiduciary crown.

Evil genius.

Still confused? Licenses and standards and commissions, lions, and tigers and bears. Oh my. That's exactly what RFAs want—to overload you with so much information that you drown in it and then quietly concede due to exhaustion.

Really, the only question that matters is: What does your RFA being a fiduciary mean for you, the retiree? Or more importantly, your retiree dollars?

In short, not much.

In practice, it is completely subjective. There is no way *anyone* can consistently differentiate a best interest recommendation from a suitable interest recommendation, or state that any commission-based investment strategy is worse than a 1% annual fee strategy.

That is crazy.

Let's start by stating the obvious. *No one* could ever say with a straight face that having an RFA like Edward Jones getting paid 1.35% to sell overpriced mutual funds could *ever* be in any human being's best interest.[86] There's a litany of newer, cheaper, better-performing and more convenient investment options. It's inarguable. An easy pivot to a robo-advisor platform could save retirees thousands of dollars each year. Does that feel like a best interest standard violation to you? But unfortunately, trillions of dollars in 1% fees are being made by your RFAs who are... fiduciaries.

Wait a second! Most RFAs made their money selling stocks for a trade commission or later on a mutual fund load commission. What is going on?

The latest workaround is for your RFA to take their fees as a percentage versus a mutual fund commission. Boom. RFAs just figured out how to beat the system again. They are now ordained to the CSRA (Church of Self-Righteous Assholes)— sorry, I meant that they are now fiduciaries—and all because of how they take money out of your accounts, not because of their services, track records, or how they plan to protect your accounts.

If it is so pointless, why do retirees keep asking the question, "Are you a fiduciary?" Simple: because every article on the Internet tells you to ask that question. Why? Because RFAs run the financial world with their trillions of fee dollars. Dollars mean marketing, articles, and influence, and they push millions of pages of content onto the web. And the only people who can answer yes to the fiduciary question are the RFAs who are— not-so-ironically—picking investments and charging you a 1% wrapper fee for the privilege.

Let me take one last shot at explaining how pointless it is to be called a "fiduciary." If you interviewed over a hundred RFAs and closed every interview with the question, "Are you an asshole?", I'm pretty darn sure every answer would be no. That's their opinion (of course), and it's inherently biased, like all opinions. That is how human minds work; we can't help it. Well, the fees an RFA chooses to charge you, the investments they sell, and the plans they recommend all come with that same bias, too.

In most RFAs' brainwashed minds, they might even believe they are taking care of their clients' best interests. That's the rub. And that's why applying subjective standards is a tricky business. Frankly, it is a pretty futile one when applied to worshiped financial deities who think they can turn water into wine.

In a nutshell, *most assholes don't know they are assholes*. So how in the world will your RFA be able to put on the brakes when they think they might cross the line between what is suitable for your retirement dollars and in your best interest, and what is not? The question is pointless.

All of this fiduciary standard BS was built to give RFAs a competitive advantage against insurance companies by blackballing commission-based products like annuities. And it was blessed by good ol' Uncle Sam.

One more thing. Did I mention that an RFA can be a fiduciary and non-fiduciary in the same meeting? I'm not joking. You can sell someone insurance as a non-fiduciary, and then turn around and charge a 1% fee as a bona fide fiduciary. You don't even have to leave the room and come back in again. Only someone in Washington DC could make this up, but it remains the "gold standard" for ensuring trust and transparency in order to convince retirees that their best interests are secured.

Not to beat a dead horse but, again, being a fiduciary reflects one passed test and an arbitrary standard under which an RFA will charge you to pick your investments. Maybe. It has nothing to do with experience, number of clients, or the services the RFA provides that actually help retirees navigate retirement risks. With a fiduciary, you are literally in the dark.

DANCING IN THE DARK

The RFA market is getting more crowded, while the dance floor gets smaller and the lights are dimming. There are newer and better retirement options appearing everywhere. But like the *Titanic*, the RFA industry is too bloated and stubborn to change course. They keep turning down the lights for retirees. Eventually, the marketing blitz will go cold as retirees wake up to the endless spin and double-talk. Buzzwords like "fiduciary" and "fee-only," along with the alphabet soup of letters like CFP, will be exposed as nothing more than empty jargon and financial theater from a desperate and dying industry. But the worst part of the coming disaster is that it is not the RFA ship that will hit the iceberg—it's yours.

The record is about to stop spinning for the RFAs of the world, and hopefully this book will help turn on the lights and get retirees off the dance floor.

Now that you can finally see, and hear yourself think again, this next chapter will show you how to fight back—using an old and new investment weapon that allows retirees to take aim at overpriced mutual funds and 1% fees.

CHAPTER 9

SECRET WEAPON

For almost four hundred years, it took fifteen to thirty seconds to fire a single flintlock shot. Samuel Colt solved that problem with the first six-shot revolver. Colt's new weapon fired quickly, but missed often. Then it happened: .44 caliber, 200-grain bullet: forty grains of black powder, 1,200 fps muzzle velocity, one-hundred-and-fifty-yard range, with a lever action discharging fifteen shots in under a minute. It was in production for fifty-two years, resulting in 720,610 units built. Buffalo Bill called it simply, "The Boss." Its official name was the Winchester New Model of 1873. Most of the world knows it better as "the gun that won the West." It changed how battles were fought—and won—for the next half a century.[87]

What if I told you there was also a perfect retirement weapon?

Like politics, brussels sprouts, religion, and former president Donald Trump, annuities provoke a visceral reaction: love or hate. No in-between. I find this both fascinating and strange for so many reasons. How could such a simple retirement tool, that is more or less a tax-deferred certificate of deposit, cause so much controversy?

To answer that question, the best thing to do is to start with the history and explain some annuity basics. Afterward, we'll look at some of the old annuity problems and the RFA smear campaign that followed. Finally, we'll unveil a newer type of annuity filling the market, which could be your secret weapon to survive retirement.

SOME HISTORY

Let's start with some fun facts. The first gasoline vehicle was invented in 1886. The first US electric vehicle was invented arguably one year later, in 1887. Yet in 2008, the US sold over 13 million gasoline vehicles and Tesla sold its first electric car.[88] That took about 120 years to happen.

There were many drivers for the imbalance, but it was primarily Henry Ford's revolutionary assembly line. It allowed him to build gasoline-powered cars at one-tenth the cost of electric cars.[89] The race was over before it started. Literally. Regardless of which energy source made the most sense, everyone got a gas-powered car for the next hundred-plus years. There were no options because there was no other real market.

On to the history of investments. The first annuity on American soil was created back in 1759.[90] It was more or less a funding mechanism to gather donations to support ministers and their families, whereas the first "modern" mutual fund rolled out around 1924.[91] We've already seen how mutual funds went from being on the verge of extinction before the 1980s to being more than a $26 *trillion*-dollar industry now. As with gasoline cars, the story was simple: mutual funds were the only thing on the menu, so that's what you got. Electric cars and annuities weren't even listed.

Gas-powered cars and mutual funds didn't dominate the market by playing nice. Big car and oil companies picked on electric cars while mutual funds did the same to annuities. They were real-life business bullies, the trust-fund kids who had everything handed to them and could buy their way out of trouble or into opportunities. Big auto and oil bought every available patent on electric and other alternative fuel ideas for a century to slow down progress and competition. In 2022, Exxon still owns nearly 13,000 active patents.[92]

The mutual fund world played their own dirty game. They couldn't just buy out all the better investment options and hide them at the patent office, so they simply tried to prohibit or discredit all competition through regulatory influence and marketing dollars. Don't ask me how the mutual fund industry and RFAs pulled it off, but they made it so that annuities weren't invited to the 401(k) party for the last forty years. That's right: you couldn't use annuities as an investment option in 401(k) plans because they were "too complicated." And despite the efforts to open doors, specifically the passing of the Secure Act in 2019 to bring more safe and guaranteed income options to retirees, less than 10% of 401(k)s have annuity options.[93] So it's no wonder they couldn't get any traction compared to the mutual funds being sold left and right. They were blackballed.

And let's not forget the shameless influence of shaping the "fiduciary" standard so it excluded anyone who sold annuities—another convenient roadblock to keep this option off retirees' radars.

The game was rigged against electric cars and annuities from the beginning. But the tides seem to be turning, and a reckoning may be just around the corner. They are both spinning their slings loaded with shiny rocks and taking aim at their respective Goliaths.

ANNUITY BASICS

Annuities are an insurance product—like life insurance policies—built by insurance companies. The most common annuities are fixed. Fixed annuities pay a fixed rate of return (i.e., 3 or 4%). Like certificates of deposit (CDs), fixed annuities do not go backward, so your principal is 100% protected. Like CDs and bonds, annuities come with a set term that can vary from one year to ten years or longer. Also like CDs and bonds, many annuities require that you hold onto them for a certain period of time, and a commission is given to the selling insurance agent by the insurance company (the fee does NOT come out of your account).[94]

However, unlike CDs and bonds, most annuities allow access to the principal every year without penalty. Retirees can take out around 10% each year without worry of a fee.

While getting access to your dollars before the end of the term of your annuity investment is certainly nice, that's not the best part. The best part is that annuities are *tax-deferred*. That means that, like your IRA, your money grows tax-free so you earn interest on interest that has not yet been taxed—then, when you take it out, you pay Uncle Sam. And when you do take out your gains, you only pay tax on the gains. That is a huge benefit when it comes to trying to limit your taxable income in retirement—and yet annuities are an often-overlooked tool.

There are also things you can add on to annuities called "riders." Think of these as similar to features on a car. The options are endless: guaranteed lifetime income, early access for long-term care costs, unlimited access to principal—the list goes on. Like car features, these riders don't come for free, and for the most part, I don't recommend them. Rider fees average between 0.25% and 1% of your principal each year, and the costs usually just aren't worth it. They add up too fast.[95]

By now, you might be scratching your head. You were told that annuities were evil incarnate—the Jason Voorhees of investments. Yet what I've just described seems like a simple and straightforward win for retirees as part of their retirement tool belt, right?

Where's the fire?

OLD ANNUITY PROBLEMS

Every family has its black sheep, they say. It's the same for annuities—although, ironically, the black sheep of the annuity family isn't even really an annuity, in my opinion. Ladies and gentlemen, meet the *variable annuity*.

They are pretty terrible all around. President Obama attempted to change certain laws that would arguably have killed variable annuities a decade ago, but couldn't get the bill to pass.

The variable annuity is more of a mutual fund than an annuity. Let me explain. Variable annuities are just a bunch of mutual funds (known as "subaccounts") with an additional insurance wrapper for marketing purposes. The first red flag is that selling them requires more than just an insurance license; it requires a Series 6. Next, they are confusing, and many retirees feel they are misrepresentative of what you get versus what you are sold. Last, the biggest problem is that they are packed to the brim with fees.[96]

The RFA sales statement that gets variable annuities in the most trouble is the fake guarantee. People are lured in with a promise of "5% guaranteed growth" every year. But it is simply not true. What they don't tell you is that 5% guaranteed growth is not *real* money. That growth only appears on a ledger account that tabulates the running tally of an income bucket. That income bucket is what is turned on for your future income stream. It is not real money you can walk away with and use. It is simply an account statement value used to calculate your annual lifetime income payment.

You do have a "real account" value number, but that account is subject to stock market ups and downs and the huge fees that come with variable annuities. The subaccount management, initial RFA commission, and additional insurance costs means the fees can regularly be 5% or more every year.

In the table below, I broke out a five-year example to show what could happen if you bought a variable annuity for $100, and how it works:

	INCOME ACCOUNT	REAL ACCOUNT	STOCK MARKET
Year 1	$105.00	$98.00	3%
Year 2	$110.25	$98.00	5%
Year 3	$115.76	$88.20	-10%
Year 4	$121.55	$83.79	0%
Year 5	$127.63	$84.63	6%

You were sold on growth: a *minimum* of 5% a year. How could you lose, when you also can participate in the upside of the market if it exceeds 5%? Sound familiar? Well, in this example the market yielded 4% positive growth over five years—and if you walked away, you would have a 16% loss. How?

Well, the real account goes up and down with the market—but it also loses 5% to fees every year. The promised "5% income account" never comes into play. It would only be applicable if you decided to turn your income account into an income stream *for the next twenty years.* All you get is the pleasure of having $6.38

($127.63 income bucket/20 years) of your own money being paid back to you for the next two decades, with no access, and no additional growth.

I can understand why you would get mad about this. I would be pissed, too. There was some serious snake oil being sold, and RFA heads should've rolled. But to set the record straight, annuities shouldn't have suffered all this bad PR. Variable annuities aren't real annuities. They are just an RFA creation to make mutual funds even more expensive and hijack the annuity name to smear. A pretty sinister move by the RFAs, right?

In better news, the world seems to be catching on, because we are seeing less and less of these terrible variable annuity products on retirees' balance sheets each year.

However, to add to Mr. Annuity's problems, the mutual fund industry had grown to trillions. It had also recognized that annuities were the only real threat to the RFA industry selling mutual funds. So it began one of the largest smear campaigns of all time. Starting in the early 2000s, the financial industry used all its size, influence, and vast wealth to flood magazines and the Internet with endless articles demonizing "annuities." There was no real explanation of why annuities are bad—just an assertion that they are. And if you had the audacity to ask why, you were directed to just listen to your fiduciary or CFP. No more questions.

This nonsense was backed up by an army of stormtroopers (RFAs) deployed to regurgitate the same slanderous lies on every retirement battlefield. It didn't matter what the articles said, the message came through loud and clear, like something out of a

George Orwell novel: "Annuities bad, mutual funds good." The average retiree didn't have any reason to believe otherwise or the information to understand how they work, so they were scared away from annuities.

THE NEW(ER) ANNUITY

An annuity is defined by Merriam-Webster as "a sum of money payable yearly or at other regular intervals."[97] This is where much of the confusion lies for retirees. In the 1980s and 1990s, almost all annuities were set up to mimic pensions. You give the insurance company a lump sum, and in return you get a certain amount back each month, with a little interest, forever. This is called "annuitizing" your annuity. Understandably, most people didn't like the idea of losing access to their principal forever. Retirees didn't just need income tools; they needed a conservative method of wealth accumulation—so the market needed to create a new tool for retirees.

From 2010 to 2020, a couple of things paved the way for this new retirement opportunity. Interest rates crashed and stayed under 5% for over a decade. With rates so low, nobody wanted to put their money into CDs or bonds. This was the opportunity annuities had been waiting for. The door flew open for a new, safe, and conservative investment alternative in the market.

The insurance companies answered the call with the fixed index annuity (FIA), an annuity that has given retirees more upside options and no downside risk. Fixed index annuities are tied to an index like the S&P 500, Dow Jones, etc., so if that index goes up, your annuity does too. If the index loses money, your floor is always zero. You will forfeit some of the unlimited upside of the stock market index, but you will have removed any chance your life savings could go backwards—the best of both worlds.

The first FIA was created in 1995, but their popularity, and the market, really took hold after 2010.[98] Retirees had finally found a tool that gave them guaranteed principal protection, participation in the market, and—one of the biggest benefits—no ongoing fees or costs. The biggest gift to the retiree population was that they no longer needed to stare at the stock ticker every day. Like the Winchester New Model 1873, the FIA was the perfect retirement weapon.

I believe that retirees would have taken this option long ago if it had been available—but alas, the only choice then was 1% annual fees with stocks, bonds, and mutual fund hot dogs.

Putting all your money on the blackjack table doesn't make sense. Nor does trying to resuscitate dead bonds and bring them back to life. The era of the investment-only approach, with the RFA chasing arbitrary returns that you don't even need to enjoy your golden years, is coming to an end. It is time for retirees to take back control of their lives and their sanity. Retirement should be the exciting part of your retirement, not your investments. Your investments should be predictable and, frankly, a little boring.

Why did you work your whole life, if not to have some time to relax and enjoy it?

We talked earlier about how the RFAs are the stormtroopers defending the Death Star (actively managed mutual funds) to exploit and control retirees.

In that analogy, the FIA is the lightsaber. It's the perfect weapon to fight back against an evil industry that has held all the cards for entirely way too long. The FIA brought annuities out of the dark ages and transformed them from a pension replacement tool to a very real wealth accumulation weapon that could finally take aim at CDs, stocks, bonds, and mutual funds.

All we need now is a hero with the courage to wield this new retirement weapon on behalf of everyday retirees!

CHAPTER 10

———

THE HERO

In one corner, a great Philistine warrior, nine feet tall, clad head to toe in shining armor and carrying a massive sword and spear. After forty consecutive days on the battlefield, mocking the enemy, he faced no challengers but one: in the other corner, the youngest of twelve sons, without armor and with no weapons other than a slingshot and five polished stones. One chance. One stone. One swing. One fallen giant. And one of history's greatest hero stories was born as David slew Goliath.

A new hero has arisen who is now taking aim at one of the industry's largest bullies of all time.

When I think of how I was raised, where I was raised, and who raised me, this story always gets me. It's the same when I watch Rocky against Ivan Drago in Russia, or Rudy chasing down his Notre Dame dream. There is just something about the underdog. The long shot. The little guy.

As you'll guess from having read this far, our Goliath is an industry that was too big, scary, wealthy, and stubborn to change. An industry that ignored what retirees needed most and abandoned them atop retirement mountain.

Once, retirees were alone and defenseless against the real risks of retirement.

Not anymore.

It's time to topple that empire. You need someone to slay the financial industry giant that has been exploiting you for too long while leaving you to find your way down retirement mountain exposed and alone.

Well, you are not alone.

Meet the Retirement Planner.

Like the Jedi wielding their lightsabers, Retirement Planners are currently few in number—but don't be fooled. They are mighty. They are the inevitable evolution from an outdated, RFA investment-only model.

The world needed a hero. And like any great story of good versus evil, necessity helped forge a new protagonist to combat a great injustice.

FOUR FOUNDING PRINCIPLES

Retirement Planners came into existence because the financial industry ignored the most dangerous threats in retirement for too long—taxes and long-term care risks—while RFAs used an overpriced and antiquated fee model to do nothing more than pick investments. Retirement Planners know that there's more to retirement than stocks and bonds. The age when RFAs get paid to gamble with other people's life savings is coming to an abrupt end.

The role of Retirement Planner was built on four guiding principles:

1. RETIREES ONLY

Retirement Planners work exclusively with people in or at retirement. The only way to effectively tailor a service and support system is to focus on a demographic whose members all have similar fears, issues, goals, and needs. You can't be everything to everyone (this is the opposite of the RFA model of servicing anyone of any age, so long as they pay their 1% each year). The only way to revolutionize retirement financial services is to put 100% of your resources into building services for retirees.

2. DEMOGRAPHIC FOCUS

The RFA industry has treated everyone the same for fifty years, from the $100,000 client to the $10 million client—charge 1% and pick investments. The Retirement Planner focuses on the $250,000–$2,500,000 client. Because they aren't paid on the value of your accounts, they can now focus on a group of retirees who all have similar issues and life goals. This allows their services to be hyper-tailored, versus trying to cram every retiree into a one-size-fits-all model.

3. ONE-ROOF APPROACH

If you've made it this far, you understand that there is more to retirement than investments. Having an action plan for taxes and long-term care is the key to any retiree's successful trip down retirement mountain. Buzzwords and a cursory conversation with a CPA or lawyer are not good enough. The empty business card referral or conference call conversation almost universally leads to the same place: nowhere. The risk is too large.

Retirement Planners renovated their house and put internal tax and legal teams under one roof. This means that Retirement Planners don't just talk about finance, tax, and legal to-dos. They don't just design plans for taxes and long-term care and throw them in a binder. They actually *execute* these plans for all of their retired clients, start to finish, with the help and expertise of all three teams: the CPA accounting team, legal team, and the Retirement Planners finance team.

4. SHEEPDOG MENTALITY

There are three types of folks in this world we all share: sheep, wolves, and sheepdogs. The sheep are many and the wolf population is growing, yet the sheepdogs remain few in number. The retirees continue to funnel into the retirement world every day, while the RFA wolves circle their new prey's retirement accounts, all in the hopes of exploiting retirees' trust.

The world is changing around us, and retirees need a new guide to protect them from the circling wolves and the risks of retirement. They need a protector. That is the mentality of every Retirement Planner. They are sheepdogs, sticking by retirees' sides to guide and protect them as they make their way down retirement mountain and, when necessary, fight off the wolves.

This mentality and sense of mission has allowed Retirement Planners to build a new and unique way of approaching not just retirement planning, but also the other services that should be included in every plan. The Retirement Planner leaves the investment-only structure behind and focuses for the first time on the largest risks of retirement: taxes, long-term care, investments, and fees.

Below is a table comparing the new approach to services created by the Retirement Planner to the old RFA approach:

SERVICES	RETIREMENT PLANNER	RFA[99]
Annual Tax Return Preparation	Yes	No
IRA Taxation—Plan Design and Implementation	Yes	No
Long-Term Care and Legacy Legal—Plan Design and Implementation	Yes	No
Old Selling Mutual Funds and Stock Investment Approach	No	Yes
New Investment Approach	Yes	No
New Fee Model	Yes	No

ANNUAL TAX RETURN PREPARATION

Filing your annual tax returns: This service may seem like a commonsense evolution, yet it remains missing from the majority of traditional RFA services. Given all the information available to your Retirement Planner, their handling of tax returns is an efficient, cost-effective way to provide retirees with tax support, guidance, and planning. This is why a Retirement Planner needs a team of CPAs to help clients navigate tax issues and get their returns filed each year.

IRA TAXATION—PLAN DESIGN AND IMPLEMENTATION

I have spent a considerable amount of time in this book discussing what will happen to your IRA dollars if you use Uncle Sam's plan. It's not a pretty picture. No retirement plan could be considered complete without a detailed plan to handle how, when, and how much money to take out of your IRA on your terms, not Uncle Sam's. But a plan on its own is like a gun with no bullets. That is why a Retirement Planner not only helps design IRA tax plans but also implements, monitors, adjusts, and *executes* your tax plan every year. Having an actual tax team in-house is imperative to make a retirement plan work and keep working.

LONG-TERM CARE—PLAN DESIGN AND IMPLEMENTATION

The largest risk in retirement requires a great plan. Nursing homes aren't getting cheaper, and the odds of needing help sooner or later are growing. Retirement Planners knew that this problem couldn't be solved by another investment sale or more insurance, so they went on the hunt. They discovered that elder-care law attorneys held an answer: asset protection trusts. Asset protection trusts are a great solution for removing assets from a retiree's name while preventing them from losing complete control and certain tax benefits. The idea is to move assets such as your home, farm, or an investment to a new asset protection trust. After a certain period of time, that asset is 100% protected from the nursing home spend-down.[100] This gives control back to retirees to customize their protection plan against long-term care—and they don't have to pay 1% a year or deal with the rising premiums of long-term care insurance to secure it.

In addition, protecting your life savings doesn't matter if they don't go where or how you want them to when you pass away. Confirming that your legacy plan is updated and reflects your wishes is very important—which is why it is part of every Retirement Planner's process.

None of this can happen for retirees efficiently, effectively, or at all without a team of estate-planning and elder-care law attorneys down the hall from your Retirement Planner. Attorneys must be involved in any cohesive retirement plan to make sure all the parts work together. Attorneys are the glue that binds it all together.

NEW INVESTMENT APPROACH

In this book, I've set out to show you all the problems with the old RFA investments Rolodex Model that has been pimped to retirees over the last fifty years. The problem Retirement Planners needed to solve was how to provide retirement-optimized investments in a way that makes sense to and for today's retiree. This new strategy required that the investments had *both* conservative and market options, but all at a cost that made better sense. The solution was to leverage and utilize new passive investing strategies such as ETFs and index funds for market participation. This allows retirees to participate in the market at a fraction of the previous cost, but without compromising performance.

With the deaths of CDs and bonds over the last ten years, a new safe haven appeared to fill the void: the fixed income annuity (FIA) we talked about in the last chapter. It has the right balance of conservative growth with no downside risk.

Most RFAs are all or nothing: either all markets and 1%, or all FIA sales. That approach doesn't work for Retirement Planners. You need both risk and safety. Every retiree is different, and you need both tools to be able to customize the right plan for retirement for everyone.

The 1980s are over. When it comes to investments, Retirement Planners are helping retirees throw away their old VHS tapes and start streaming.

NEW FEE MODEL

Wow. Fees were a huge and costly problem in the RFA model. If you don't know why, well, you clearly skipped to the end of this book.

You now know that lazily charging 1% for virtually nothing but picking some stock is devoid of any meaningful value proposition or correlation to your planning. That is why Retirement Planners put *your* money where their mouth is. Retirement Planners charge a transparent flat fee of $3,000 each year.[101] That's it, no matter how many zeroes are in your accounts.

That pays for your annual tax return, the design and execution of your tax plan by CPAs, the design and execution of your legal plan by attorneys, retirement-optimized investment allocation and management, and annual income/expense forecast documentation (looking backward and forward). Of course, it also gives you access to both the tax and legal teams throughout your entire retirement, rather than your having to pay a floating fee hidden on your statements that is based on a percentage of your total assets.

Now you have a list of services and a flat fee to compare with RFAs. You can put them side by side and decide for yourself whether the cost of a Retirement Planner and their team of CPAs and attorneys is worth $3,000.

THE SHEEPDOG

The mission of every Retirement Planner is simple: to protect retirees. That could be protecting them from RFAs, or from the inherent risks of retirement, or both. The protection-first approach allows Retirement Planners to tailor services and support to fit the goals of retirees and alleviate their greatest fear: running out of money.

Providing actionable services means that Retirement Planners do what they say, and do it all under one roof, at one simple-to-understand fee.

It's hard to understand why anyone would want to go back to rewinding VHS tapes after experiencing the ease of pushing a button from their couch and streaming their favorite TV show whenever they want. That's also *exactly* how I feel about using a financial advisor.

Why would you continue to pay 1% for an RFA to pick investments and ignore the rest of retirement, regardless of the letters they have next to their name on their website or business cards or who they golf with on Saturdays? Retirement Planners are the future, whether RFAs are ready to go away or not. It is too late for them. The dam is broken and the information is out there. We just need people to continue to share it with their friends, family, and loved ones.

Together, we won't just fight back against a $26 trillion industry that has exploited retirees at every turn; we can win.[102] Retirees can come away with the ultimate victory for themselves *and* future retirees.

And if we all do it together, we can change the financial world.

Well, there you have it. You made it. I started off by explaining how retirees fell into this bear trap. I went on to show you how the world changed and RFAs refused to change along with it. And I showed you how retirees can now get out of the trap and move forward with a new guide and protector, a Retirement Planner.

Most importantly, and as promised, I showed you why you should fire your financial advisor.

I rest my case.

APPENDIX A

———

SHOULD I FIRE MY FINANCIAL ADVISOR?

Congratulations—you made it through step one! You've finished this book. Now you realize that some things just don't add up when it comes to who has been entrusted with your life savings. There are some serious issues out there.

So if your head is spinning, don't worry. You are not alone. I've told this story to many retirees face to face, and you likely have a lot of questions:

- Can the things this guy wrote be true?
- Did my RFA reallocate my assets to safer investments at retirement?
- How much of my money could go backwards?
- What am I paying my financial advisor?
- What am I paying for the investments they sold me?
- Why don't I have a tax plan for my IRA?
- Do I have a plan for long-term care?

- What services does my financial advisor provide besides selling investments?

And of course, the big question that combines all of these concerns: Should I really fire my financial advisor?

Next up is finding answers to those questions. We're talking about your life savings. I think it's reasonable to assume that you owe it to yourself and your family to take the time to do some tire kicking and make sure you feel confident that your money is in the right hands.

There are two easy ways to find reliable answers to your questions.

Option 1—Visit www.fireyourfinancialadvisor.com.

This easy-to-complete, printable form will provide you with a list of vital questions that every retiree should ask, and know the answers to, when it comes to the professional entrusted with protecting your life's savings. Armed with these questions and answers, you can sit down with your financial advisor and get all the information you need to understand what they are doing—or failing to do—to protect you, and what they are charging you for their services and investments.

Option 2—Go to www.getyourroadmap.com.

We get it. Sitting down and re-interviewing your financial advisor is tough. You've built a personal relationship with this person, so challenging them about what they actually do, or don't do, and how much they charge you can be awkward and uncomfortable.

Don't put your head in the sand. Don't ignore it, because it is just too important. You don't have to do this by yourself, however. Our Retirement Planners can do it for you. If you hop on that website and provide us with the requested information, we will provide you with the expert attorneys, CPAs, and Retirement Planners who will find answers to all your questions without you ever having to have a conversation with your financial advisor. They won't even know we are helping you. At the end, you will walk away with a customized Roadmap for Retirement®. And if you mention that you read this book, we will do it at no cost.

This roadmap will give you the data you need to understand your position, see what is missing, and identify the largest risks to you and your family in retirement.

Whether you use Option 1 or Option 2, you will end up in a position to confidently decide if you should *Fire Your Financial Advisor*.

HOW TO FIRE YOUR FINANCIAL ADVISOR

Well, you made the decision. Your financial advisor has to go. That leaves just one last step: actually doing it. You need to deliver the news to someone with whom you have probably built a relationship. For most retirees, this is not easy. In the words of Neil Sedaka, "Breaking up is hard to do." And that is exactly what you are doing.

Over the years, my team has coached thousands of retirees on how to make this transition go smoothly. So here are five tips to make things easier when it's time to deliver the pink slip.

1. SHORT AND SWEET

The most common mistake retirees make is to try to explain or, worse, *justify* their decision to move on. This will never end well. Your financial advisor is a professional confuser and relationship manager. They are ready for you, and even readier to play defense. They aren't going to congratulate you and wish you luck on your smart retirement decision. Instead, they are going to request meetings and calls and do anything they can to keep you as a client. They are in panic mode because they are about to take a pay cut if you remove your account and they lose their 1% fee.

Your financial advisor will tell you they can actually provide all the same services you mention, or they will offer to revisit their fees, or they will discredit your Retirement Planner.

The reality is that if they could have done those things for you, they already would have.

As a business owner, I have had to part ways with hundreds of employees, and the strategy is always the same: "We are going to have to let you go today." We don't go into the why or answer detailed questions; if we have gotten to the point of firing someone, the time for that is long past. If we did open that door, it would inevitably lead to excuses, defensiveness, and anger, and none of those would get us anywhere apart from back to the decision we already made. Our team's policy is to not answer any questions, simply reiterate that the decision is made, and wish them luck.

The same goes for firing your financial advisor. Do not explain anything. This is your money. You have paid them (probably too much already) for their services, and you do not owe them anything else at this point. Keep it short and sweet:

> "Dear Financial Advisor, thank you so much for everything you have done for our family. We appreciate it, but we have decided that we are going in a different direction. Regarding moving our savings, please facilitate any account transfer requests going forward to my new Retirement Planner's company. Thanks again."

Do not answer any questions regarding the why or where. That is a trap. You will feel an urge to explain your decision in the hopes that will help them understand or agree; it will not. Trying to explain asset protection trusts, tax maps, or how a Retirement Planner's services are different from a financial advisor's will not end well. It will only lead to confusion. Of course, confusion is exactly what your financial advisor wants, because they are desperately trying to do anything to halt the termination process of their 1% fee.

The simple reply to any question is always the same:

"Thank you again for everything, but we have made our decision."

That applies to *anything* a financial advisor says going forward to thwart your decision. After the second or third time you repeat it, they will get the idea and it will end all the badgering and follow-ups during your transition period.

2. IT'S JUST BUSINESS

Treat your retirement accounts like your own family business. Businesses change vendors all the time. Prices and services change constantly, as do the needs of the business. Why should it be any different when it comes to your life savings? You used your financial advisor to get to the top of retirement mountain, but now you need a different guide, with different tools, to get you down.

Your financial advisor will try to make it personal. It is not personal. It is simply a smart business decision. Your financial advisor doesn't have the right tools and teams to ensure that you can make it safely down the mountain.

3. THEY ARE *NOT* YOUR FRIEND

This is particularly hard to accept. Your RFA neighbor, deacon at church, or guy who grabs coffee with you once a month is probably *not* your friend. That person is being paid to manage and maintain your relationship, even though they're likely great at making their friendship seem genuine. I know this isn't fun to read or hear, but ask yourself this question: "If I left my financial advisor tomorrow, would they still call, grab lunch or vacation with me, or remain a part of my life?" I think most of you know the answer. Friendship should not come with a quarterly statement.

Financial advisors are in the business of making you feel connected and comfortable, which leads to trust, then loyalty, and eventually to you never questioning them about fees, poor market performance, or other important missing services—which ultimately leads to you never leaving them.

What other friends in your life cost you 1% of your life savings every year?

4. IT'S *YOUR* MONEY

It's your money, not your financial advisor's. But the system is set up the opposite way so that you are made to feel guilty about spending it or even thinking about spending it. You have to ask someone's permission to take it out. That doesn't feel right, does it? What's the point of working your whole life if you can't enjoy what you worked to accumulate?

This is part of the financial advisor's master plan. They scare you by bringing up how they are doing everything for your benefit so you don't run out of money. It's bullshit. You aren't running out of money. They just don't want to take a pay cut while you enjoy your life savings more and more every year.

It's a little like Stockholm Syndrome. Your financial advisor has controlled and dictated your retirement for so long—kidnapping your retirement decisions—that you may feel paralyzed and guilty spending your own money or making decisions about your retirement dollars.

It is not lost on me that this is a real relationship that could have been built over the last twenty years. But this all comes down to a decision. You can either allow someone to continue to kidnap your retirement decisions and dollars because you feel bad about stopping them—or you can remember that this is *your* money, not theirs, and deliver that pink slip.

5. RETIREMENT PLANNER SUPPORT
You are not alone.

If you make the huge decision to entrust your life savings with another person and firm, then this new guide should be shoulder-to-shoulder with you every step of the way to support and assist you in making the transition easier. In many cases, you don't need to say anything to your previous financial advisor if you don't want to have that final "goodbye" conversation. Your Retirement Planner can do all the necessary paperwork without you ever having to talk to your previous financial advisor, if that's what you prefer.

Retirement Planners are in the business of working only with retirees, so every client in their system has transitioned over from a previous financial advisor. That means that Retirement Planners know the lay of the land, and will be by your side to take as much of the burden off of you as you desire when it comes to transitioning your retirement savings.

So if you are using a Retirement Planner for your retirement dollars, go for it. You are making a great decision.

Like jumping into a lake on a cold morning, or ripping off a Band-Aid, you just have to just do it.

Go out and fire your financial advisor.

ACKNOWLEDGMENTS

A special thanks to you for reading this book. As I shared with you right at the start, my goal for writing my first book was to make it interesting and compelling enough to read cover to cover. That's what you've done, so thank you. I hope you have enjoyed reading it as much as I enjoyed writing it.

I am a lucky guy.

Amazing kids: My Lilly inspires me every day with her wit, composure, and drive at the age of just nine—she is so freaking serious, and funny. I see so much of myself in her, yet she is better than me in so many ways. She is my best friend. And my crazy twins Lola and Louie inspire me with their two-year-old, endless curiosity about life. They are a fountain of happiness, delivering smiles when the walls of life are crashing in. I love all three of my maniacs.

Amazing parents: Big John and Sandy are responsible for me. They taught me how to treat people. How to put in a hard day's work. And they continue to support me at every turn and show me what it feels like to be loved unconditionally. Thank you, Mom and Dad—words can't describe my appreciation. I love you, Mama and Pops.

Amazing team: The loyalty, grit, and trust of my AlerStallings and Golden Reserve work families are why I have been able to keep going for the last twelve-plus years. They are the engine that never stops for me, my teammates, and all the retirees we guide out there. Without each of them, this book and our companies' successes would not be possible, and they are too numerous to name here, but Mr. Tim Stallings needs to be mentioned. He has been there with me since day one, risking it all on a dream. Tim has been a great friend and a true partner in crime from the beginning. Love you, Timmy, and of course the rest of our squad.

Amazing partner: Mr. Justin Spring gets his own shout-out. Justin is not only our president, but the other half of our companies, offsetting my impulsiveness with his deliberation. His balance supplied the necessary rocket fuel for Golden Reserve to lift off. He is the reason this book was written. He helped me believe that we had a story worth telling, and wouldn't leave me alone until I put the damn thing into writing. He has been the sounding board I have always needed—a true entrepreneur, marketing genius, and, most importantly, a fucking great friend (Justin said I couldn't use the f-word in this book. Ha! Snuck it in). Love you, buddy.

Amazing wife: Last but certainly not least, I am grateful to and for my wife Fernanda. She has been my rock, biggest fan, protector, and North Star for my entire adult life. She has never left my side no matter how crazy or stupid I acted, and man, am I crazy. And she has relentlessly trusted and supported me in every new business triumph and failure. (Note her solo parenting on the endless weekend mornings I squeezed in over the course of this last year, writing this book.) She is my everything. Thank you, baby, and *eu te amo, meu amor.*

NOTES

1   Richard Fry, "The Pace of Boomer Retirements Has Accelerated in the Past Year," Pew Research Center, November 9, 2020, https://www.pewresearch.org/fact-tank/2020/11/09/the-pace-of-boomer-retirements-has-accelerated-in-the-past-year/.

2   Joanna Short, "Economic History of Retirement in the United States," ed. Robert Whaples, EH.net, September 30, 2002, https://eh.net/encyclopedia/economic-history-of-retirement-in-the-united-states/.

3   Andrew Noymer, "Figure 2: Life Expectancy in the USA, 1900–98: Men and Women," Berkeley.edu, accessed November 7, 2022, https://u.demog.berkeley.edu/~andrew/1918/figure2.html.

4   Christopher Klein, "How Much Did the First-Ever Social Security Check Pay Out?" History.com, May 14, 2019, https://www.history.com/news/first-social-security-check.

5   Short, "Economic History of Retirement"; Noymer, "Life Expectancy."

6   Federal Reserve Bank of St. Louis, "Gross Domestic Product (GDP)," Federal Reserve Economic Data, last modified October 27, 2022, https://fred.stlouisfed.org/series/GDP#.

7   Federal Reserve Bank of St. Louis, "GDP."

8   Roxy Simons, "Is the Last 'Blockbuster" Still Open? The Truth about Netflix Show Location," *Newsweek*, November 3, 2022, https://www.newsweek.com/last-blockbuster-still-open-truth-about-netflix-show-location-1756025; Sharon Oliver, "'The Last Blockbuster': Rewinding to Another Era," Culture Sonar, January 2, 2021, https://www.culturesonar.com/the-last-blockbuster-rewinding-to-another-era; Andy Ash, "The Rise and Fall of Blockbuster and How It's Surviving with Just One Store Left," Insider, last modified August 12, 2020, https://www.businessinsider.com/the-rise-and-fall-of-blockbuster-video-streaming-2020-1; Frank Olito, "The Rise and Fall of Blockbuster," Insider, last modified August 20, 2020, https://www.businessinsider.com/rise-and-fall-of-blockbuster.

9   Ash, "The Rise and Fall of Blockbuster and How It's Surviving with Just One Store Left."

10 Sean Collins et al., *2022 Investment Company Fact Book: A Review of Trends and Activities in the Investment Company Industry* (Washington, DC: Investment Company Institute, 2022), 22, https://eh.net/encyclopedia/economic-history-of-retirement-in-the-united-states/.

11 Melissa Phipps, "The History of Pension Plans in the U.S.", The Balance, updated October 14, 2021, https://www.thebalancemoney.com/the-history-of-the-pension-plan-2894374.

12 Kathleen Elkins, "A Brief History of the 401(k), Which Changed How Americans Retire," CNBC, January 4, 2017, https://www.cnbc.com/2017/01/04/a-brief-history-of-the-401k-which-changed-how-americans-retire.html.

13 "401(k) Plan Research: FAQs," Investment Company Institute, October 11, 2021, https://www.ici.org/faqs/faq/401k/faqs_401k.

14 John Csiszar, "The Pension Is Dead—Is the 401(k) Next?" Yahoo! Finance, January 3, 2022, https://finance.yahoo.com/news/pension-dead-401-k-next-120110699.html?guccounter=1.

15 "Federal Funds Rate—62 Year Historical Chart," Macrotrends, last modified November 4, 2022, https://www.macrotrends.net/2015/fed-funds-rate-historical-chart.

16 "Dow Jones—DJIA—100 Year Historical Chart," Macrotrends, last modified November 7, 2022, https://www.macrotrends.net/1319/dow-jones-100-year-historical-chart.

17 A white squall, if you're unfamiliar with the expression, is a very rare phenomenon on the high seas during which air pushed down by pressure in the atmosphere has nowhere to go when it meets the ocean so is rerouted outward, causing hundred-knot winds full of water. Very few humans have ever witnessed one.

18 As of September 1, 2022, per https://insurance.ohio.gov/static/Agent/Documents/804+OH+INS+UCS.pdf.

19 As of September 1, 2022, per https://www.finra.org/registration-exams-ce/qualification-exams/series65.

20 As of September 1, 2022, per https://generalcontractorlicenseguide.com/ohio-plumbing-license/.

21 As of September 1, 2022, per https://ohiodnr.gov/buy-and-apply/hunting-fishing-boating/fishing-resources/fishing-licenses.

22 Caroline Banton, "Double Dipping," Investopedia, last modified April 25, 2022, https://www.investopedia.com/terms/d/doubledipping.asp.

23 Brian Reid, "The 1990s: A Decade of Expansion and Change in the U.S. Mutual Fund Industry," *Perspective* 6, no. 3 (July 2000): 1–20, https://www.ici.org/doc-server/pdf%3Aper06-03.pdf.

24 William H. Jones, "U.S. Mutual Funds Are Alive, Well And Looking Good," *The Washington Post*, January 5, 1981, https://www.washingtonpost.com/archive/business/1981/01/05/us-mutual-funds-are-alive-well-and-looking-good/659e2fb3-a74a-4a56-b878-74e3c22d6c39/.

25 Michael Coyne, "Ending a NYSE Tradition: The 1975 Unraveling of Broker's Fixed Commissions and Its Long Term Impact on Financial Advertising," *Essays in Economic and Business* 25 (2007): 131–141, https://digitalcommons.fairfield.edu/cgi/viewcontent.cgi?article=1102&context=business-facultypubs.

26 Charles M. Jones, "A Century of Stock Market Liquidity and Trading Costs," (master's thesis, Columbia University, 2002), SSRN, http://dx.doi.org/10.2139/ssrn.313681.

27 Kent Thune, "Basics on Mutual Fund Fees, Loads, and Expenses," The Balance, last modified March 2, 2022, https://www.thebalancemoney.com/basics-on-mutual-fund-fees-loads-and-expenses-2466616.

28 Sit Mutual Funds, Inc., "Distribution Plan (Rule 12b-1 Plan)," U.S. Securities and Exchange Commission, March 20, 2015, https://www.sec.gov/Archives/edgar/data/877880/000119312515106487/d895701dex99m.htm.

29 Caleb Silver, "The Top 25 Economies in the World," Investopedia, last modified September 1, 2022, https://www.investopedia.com/insights/worlds-top-economies/; Sean Collins et al., *2022 Investment Company Fact Book: A Review of Trends and Activities in the Investment Company Industry* (Washington, DC: Investment Company Institute, 2022), 22, https://www.icifactbook.org/pdf/2022_factbook.pdf.

30 Vartanig G. Vartan, "Mutual Funds' Historic Boom," *New York Times*, December 17, 1985, https://www.nytimes.com/1985/12/17/business/mutual-funds-historic-boom.html.

31 "Occupational Employment and Wage Statistics: OEWS Data: May 2021," U.S. Bureau of Labor Statistics, last modified March 31, 2022, https://www.bls.gov/oes/current/oes_nat.htm; "OEWS Data: 2001," U.S. Bureau of Labor Statistics, accessed November 7, 2022, https://www.bls.gov/oes/tables.htm.

32 "OEWS Data: May 2020," U.S. Bureau of Labor Statistics, last modified March 31, 2021, https://www.bls.gov/oes/2020/may/oes_nat.htm; "OEWS Data: 2000," U.S. Bureau of Labor Statistics, accessed November 7, 2022, https://www.bls.gov/oes/tables.htm.

33 Michele Alexander et al., *Life Insurers Fact Book 2019* (Washington, DC: American Council of Life Insurers, 2019), 6, https://www.acli.com/-/media/ACLI/Files/Fact-Books-Public/2019FLifeInsurersFactBook.ashx?la=en.

34 Vartan, "Historic Boom."

35 Collins et al., *2022 Fact Book*, 21–22.

36 "Edward Jones Email Communications Terms and Conditions," Edward Jones, accessed November 7, 2022, https://www.edwardjones.com/us-en/disclosures/email.

37 "Share Class Pricing Details—American Funds," Capital Group, accessed November 7, 2022, https://www.capitalgroup.com/individual/what-we-offer/share-class-information/share-class-pricing.html.

38 Vartan, "Historic Boom."

39 "Total Assets of Retirement Annuities in the United States from 2000 to 2021," Statista, September 8, 2022, https://www.statista.com/statistics/188002/retirement-annuities-total-assets-in-the-us-since-2000/.

40 The fiduciary standard will be discussed more in Chapter 8, but in short, if an advisor receives a commission, they can't be a fiduciary. However, if the advisor charges a 1% fee and gets certain licenses, they can be a fiduciary. Strange, but that is basically the rule.

41 US Securities and Exchange Commission, "Edward Jones to Pay $75 Million to Settle Revenue Sharing Charges," news release no. 2004-177, last modified December 22, 2004, https://www.sec.gov/news/press/2004-177.htm.

42 "Revenue Sharing, Shareholder Accounting, Inforce Contract and Unit Investment Trust Additional Compensation," Edward Jones, accessed November 7, 2022, https://www.edwardjones.com/us-en/disclosures/revenue-sharing.

43 "Number of Active and Passive Mutual Funds in the United States from 2000 to 2021," Statista, July 4, 2022, https://www.statista.com/statistics/1263885/number-active-passive-mutual-funds-usa/.

44 Liz Knueven and Rickie Houston, "The Average Stock Market Return over the Past 10 Years," Insider, last modified May 26, 2022, https://www.businessinsider.com/personal-finance/average-stock-market-return.

45 Ben Carlson, "How Long Does it Take to Make Your Money Back After a Bear Market?" *A Wealth of Common Sense* (blog), March 13, 2020, https://awealthofcommonsense.com/2020/03/how-long-does-it-take-to-make-your-money-back-after-a-bear-market/.

46 Arthur Conan Doyle, *The Hound of the Baskervilles* (London: George Newnes, Limited, 1902), 52.

47 "11 Facts about Literacy in America," DoSomething.org, accessed November 7, 2022, https://www.dosomething.org/us/facts/11-facts-about-literacy-america.

48 Morgan Housel, The Psychology of Money: Timeless Lessons on Wealth, Greed, and Happiness (Petersfield: Harriman House, 2020), 45.

49 Charles MacKay, *Extraordinary Popular Delusions and the Madness of Crowds* (New York: Harmony Books, 1980).

50 "Edward Jones among Fortune 500 for 10th Consecutive Year," Edward Jones, accessed November 7, 2022, https://www.edwardjones.com/us-en/why-edward-jones/news-media/press-releases/2022-fortune-500-ranking.

51 U.S. Securities and Exchange Commission, "Edward Jones to Pay $75 Million to Settle Revenue Sharing Charges," news release no. 2004-177, last modified December 22, 2004, https://www.sec.gov/news/press/2004-177.htm.

52 Associated Press, "Edward Jones to Settle Class Actions," *Los Angeles Times*, September 1, 2006, https://www.latimes.com/archives/la-xpm-2006-sep-01-fi-wrap1.1-story.html.

53 Daren Fonda, "Reverse-Churning Lawsuit against Edward Jones Is Revived," *Barron's*, August 7, 2019, https://www.barrons.com/articles/edward-jones-lawsuit-revived-51565191806.

54 Hunter Kuffel, "Edward Jones Financial Advisor Review," SmartAsset, last modified July 27, 2022, https://smartasset.com/financial-advisor/edward-jones-wealth-management-review.

55 See www.americanfunds.com.

56 Kuffel, "Edward Jones Review."

57 Amanda Gengler, "Edward Jones Review," Magnify Money, last modified May 23, 2022, https://www.magnifymoney.com/investing/ria/edward-jones/.

58 Jennifer Corbett, "Criminal Fraud Laws," Legal Match, last modified March 18, 2021, https://www.legalmatch.com/law-library/article/criminal-fraud.html.

59 Patrick Kariuki, "How and When Did Netflix Start? A Brief History of the Company," Muo, last modified July 7, 2022, https://www.makeuseof.com/how-when-netflix-start-brief-company-history; Julia Stoll, "Quarterly Netflix Paid Streaming Subscribers in the U.S. and Canada 2013–2022," Statista, October 19, 2022.

60 "Nickelodeon (America's First Commercial Movie Theater), Pittsburgh," GPSMYCITY, accessed November 7, 2022, https://www.gpsmycity.com/attractions/nickelodeon-(americas-first-commercial-movie-theater)-25303.html.

61 Dana Feldman, "How Netflix Is Changing the Future of Movie Theaters," *Forbes*, July 28, 2019, https://www.forbes.com/sites/danafeldman/2019/07/28/how-netflix-is-changing-the-future-of-movie-theaters/?sh=2c9a39ac5f46.

62　"13 Powerful Facts You Didn't Know About Hoover Dam," *Gray Line Las Vegas Blog*, May 9, 2022, https://graylinelasvegas.com/blog/8-powerful-facts-you-didnt-know-about-hoover-dam; "Hoover Dam," Water Education Foundation, accessed November 21, 2022, https://www.watereducation.org/aquapedia/hoover-dam.

63　Tatiana Schlossberg, "The State of Publishing: Literacy Rates," McSweeney's, February 7, 2011, https://www.mcsweeneys.net/articles/literacy-rates.

64　This 40% is based on the assumption your IRA dollars will be taxed at the higher federal and state income rates if you don't have a tax plan for how to take your money out of your IRA.

65　This 48% represents the S&P 500 losses from August 28, 2008, to March 9, 2009: Gerald P. Dwyer, "Stock Prices in the Financial Crisis," *Notes from the Vault*, Federal Reserve Bank of Atlanta, September 2009, https://www.atlantafed.org/cenfis/publications/notesfromthevault/0909.

66　Gutenberg died broke, believing his printing press was a failure.

67　Sean Collins et al., *2022 Investment Company Fact Book: A Review of Trends and Activities in the Investment Company Industry* (Washington, DC: Investment Company Institute, 2022), 117, https://www.icifactbook.org/pdf/2022_factbook.pdf; William H. Jones, "U.S. Mutual Funds Are Alive, Well and Looking Good," *The Washington Post*, January 5, 1981, https://www.washingtonpost.com/archive/business/1981/01/05/us-mutual-funds-are-alive-well-and-looking-good/659e2fb3-a74a-4a56-b878-74e3c22d6c39/.

68　"Mutual Funds—Statistics & Facts," Statista, June 7, 2022, https://www.statista.com/topics/1441/mutual-funds/#dossierKeyfigures.

69　Burton G. Malkiel, *A Random Walk down Wall Street* (New York: W. W. Norton & Company, 2011), 157–162.

70　Paul A. Merriman, "The Genius of John Bogle in 9 Quotes," Market Watch, November 25, 2016, https://www.marketwatch.com/story/the-genius-of-john-bogle-in-9-quotes-2016-11-23.

71　John Edwards, "How Vanguard Index Funds Work," Investopedia, last modified September 28, 2022, https://www.investopedia.com/articles/investing/111715/how-vanguard-index-funds-work.asp.

72　Stephen D. Simpson, "A Brief History of Exchange-Traded Funds," Investopedia, January 31, 2022, https://www.investopedia.com/articles/exchangetradedfunds/12/brief-history-exchange-traded-funds.asp.

73　Tom Maloney and Hema Parmar, "Five Hedge Fund Heads Made More than $1 Billion Each Last Year," *Bloomberg*, February 11, 2020, https://www.bloomberg.com/news/articles/2020-02-11/five-hedge-fund-heads-earned-more-than-1-billion-each-last-year.

74 Nadia Ahmad, "What Is the Average Investment Management Fee?" SmartAsset, March 31, 2022, https://smartasset.com/investing/what-is-the-average-investment-management-fee.

75 Assumes a twenty-five-year retirement.

76 Barbara Friedberg, "Top-10 Robo-Advisors by Assets under Management," *Forbes*, last modified July 9, 2022, https://www.forbes.com/advisor/investing/top-robo-advisors-by-aum/.

77 Lindsay Modglin, "Long-Term Care Statistics 2022," *The Checkup* (blog), February 15, 2022, https://www.singlecare.com/blog/news/long-term-care-statistics/.

78 Jeff Hoyt, "Nursing Home Costs in 2022," SeniorLiving.org, last modified October 25, 2022, https://www.seniorliving.org/nursing-homes/costs/.

79 Howard Gleckman, "Who Owns Long-Term Care Insurance?" *Forbes*, August 18, 2016, https://www.forbes.com/sites/howardgleckman/2016/08/18/who-owns-long-term-care-insurance/?sh=6aff66d62f05.

80 "Retirement Topics—Required Minimum Distributions (RMDs)," IRS.gov, last modified September 23, 2022, https://www.irs.gov/retirement-plans/plan-participant-employee/retirement-topics-required-minimum-distributions-rmds; "Life Expectancy (years) in United States of America," Data Commons: Place Explorer, accessed November 21, 2022, https://datacommons.org/place/country/USA?utm_medium=explore&mprop=lifeExpectancy&popt=Person&hl=en.

81 Jeff Camarda, "America's Broken Financial Advisor Promise—What's Wrong with the CFP Board & Why You'd Better Check Twice before Trusting a Certified Financial Planner," *Forbes*, September 23, 2019, https://www.forbes.com/sites/jeffcamarda/2019/09/23/americas-broken-financial-advisor-promisewhats-wrong-with-the-cfp-board--why-youd-better-check-twice-before-trusting-a-certified-financial-planner/?sh=857786d37123.

82 Kaplan Financial Education, "How to Become a CFP Professional," Kaplan, April 1, 2021, https://www.kaplanfinancial.com/resources/getting-started/how-to-become-a-cfp-professional.

83 Camarda, "Broken Promise."

84 Camarda, "Broken Promise."

85 CAUTION: The specifics and application of the fiduciary standard are subjects of ongoing debate. This summary is my view and, I believe, a view shared by most folks in the financial industry.

86 Hunter Kuffel, "Edward Jones Financial Advisor Review," SmartAsset, last modified July 27, 2022, https://smartasset.com/financial-advisor/edward-jones-wealth-management-review.

87 David E. Petzal, "The Gun that Won the West," *Field & Stream*, January 5, 2021, https://www.fieldandstream.com/story/guns/winchester-model-1873-gun-that-won-the-west/.

88 Jim Henry, "U.S. Auto Sales Fell 18 Percent in 2008," CBS News, last modified January 5, 2009, https://www.cbsnews.com/news/us-auto-sales-fell-18-percent-in-2008.

89 Kevin A. Wilson, "Worth the Watt: A Brief History of the Electric Car, 1830 to Present," *Car and Driver*, August 17, 2022, https://www.caranddriver.com/features/g15378765/worth-the-watt-a-brief-history-of-the-electric-car-1830-to-present.

90 "A Brief History of Annuities," Due, accessed November 7, 2022, https://due.com/annuity/a-brief-history-of-annuities.

91 James McWhinney, "A Brief History of the Mutual Fund," Investopedia, last modified January 29, 2022, https://www.investopedia.com/articles/mutualfund/05/mfhistory.asp.

92 Exxon Mobil Corporation, "Annual Report Pursuant to Section 13 OR 15(d) of the Securities Exchange Act of 1934, Form 10-K, for the Fiscal Year Ended December 31, 2018," U.S. Securities and Exchange Commission, February 27, 2019, https://www.sec.gov/Archives/edgar/data/34088/000003408819000010/xom10k2018.htm.

93 Sarah O'Brien, "The Secure Act May Flood Your 401(k) with Annuities. Here's What You Should Know," CNBC, July 3, 2019, https://www.cnbc.com/2019/07/03/if-annuities-come-to-your-401k-savings-plan-heres-what-to-know.html.

94 This is the opposite of RFA and mutual fund fees, in which your account value decreases after every commission or annual fee is charged.

95 Elaine Silvestrini, "Annuity Fees and Commissions," Annuity.org, last modified September 8, 2022, https://www.annuity.org/annuities/fees-and-commissions.

96 Eve Kaplan, "9 Reasons You Need to Avoid Variable Annuities," *Forbes*, July 2, 2012, https://www.forbes.com/sites/feeonlyplanner/2012/07/02/9-reasons-you-need-to-avoid-variable-annuities/?sh=196c98a55f19.

97 *Merriam-Webster*, s.v. "annuity (n.)," accessed November 7, 2022, https://www.merriam-webster.com/dictionary/annuity.

98 Cathy DeWitt Dunn, "The Evolution & History of Fixed Index Annuities," Annuity Watch USA, accessed November 7, 2022, https://www.annuitywatchusa.com/the-evolution-history-of-fixed-index-annuities.

99 This services analysis was based on reviewing Edward Jones, Fisher Investments, Ameriprise, and Edelman Financial based on the summary of services of each on www.smartasset.com.

100 As of July 2022, in Ohio, the amount of time used by the Department of Job and Family Services is five years.

101 This $3,000 fee is based on Golden Reserve's full-service retirement planner package, as of July 2022.

102 Sean Collins et al., *2022 Investment Company Fact Book: A Review of Trends and Activities in the Investment Company Industry* (Washington, DC: Investment Company Institute, 2022), 22, https://www.icifactbook.org/pdf/2022_factbook.pdf.